*Call Back The Lovely April*

# Call Back The Lovely April

Edith Breeden

Kineton: The Roundwood Press
1972

Set in 'Monotype' Bembo series 428 and printed by Gordon Norwood
at The Roundwood Press, Kineton, in the County of Warwick

*Made and Printed in Great Britain*

*To Joy and Bill
and with acknowledgement
to P. M. T.*

# Contents

# 1. Arrival

A 'TINY FEATHER from the wing of love' fluttered into a Lewes household, towards the end of the nineteenth Century. This was Mama's euphemistic way of announcing my birth to Annie, my sister, who was thirteen. Annie's knowledge of matters connected with birth was fragmentary and confused. She had long discarded the idea that the doctor's black bag, or the gooseberry bush, were the magical repositories of these new arrivals. Now, a fluttering feather seemed even more absurd—more dust thrown in her eyes. Annie longed for a clue to the mystery, but she knew of no authentic source of information.

No speculation on the subject troubled the mind of Harry, my brother, who was eleven. He received the news that he had a new sister with nonchalance. The arrival of a kitten or a puppy would have been far more exciting.

It was not until I had emerged from the cocoon-like torpor of early infancy that Harry's interest quickened, and he found my efforts to talk and walk, a source of amusement and delight. With the rest of the family, he hailed as a major achievement my first tottering steps, and was full of excitement when the first intelligible word emerged from my baby jargon.

In later years Annie often considered it her duty to reprimand me for childish misdemeanours. She usually ended the scolding, by declaring that I had always been thoroughly spoiled as a baby.

This spoiling left no memory with me, for I did not become aware of myself as an entity until I had passed my second birthday. Then, another feather fluttered into the nest, and I ceased to be the centre of attraction. I resented this demanding intruder, and felt forlorn when I saw my baby brother, Stanley, being cradled in Mama's arms. The new toys which had been given to me were no comfort. The pride I had felt in having a real bed of my own in Annie's room, evaporated.

I longed to be back in my cot by the side of Mama's bed, where Stanley now slept. No longer could I creep each morning into the big feather bed with its shiny brass knobs to snuggle down cosily into its warmth and comfort.

To ease my hurt, I turned to Harry and followed him like a shadow, whenever he was at home. When Harry was busy in the garden, I tried to help him. My hands and clothes, as well as the garden, suffered from my exertions but he was very patient.

Perhaps his patience was taxed to the limit, for he tactfully persuaded Mama to let me have a small portion of her flower border for my own. Harry and Mama were both keen gardeners but Papa and Annie both disliked gardening. Papa often said that his fingers were not green, like Mama's. This mystified me for I could not see that Mama's fingers differed in any way from my own.

Harry soon cleared the small patch allotted to me. It was to be all mine. I could dig where I liked. With a small spade and rake, I was soon at work. Each day I dug diligently until it was time for seeds to be sown. With Harry, I set off gaily to the seed shop. Confronted with the galaxy of colour on the packets, I wanted to plant them all but Harry wisely chose a few for me. I tugged at his hand all the way home in my hurry to plant immediately these seeds of Virginia Stock, Marigolds and Forget-me-nots, in my very own garden.

Each day I viewed the small plot expectantly. More than once I surreptitiously dug up a small portion to see how things were progressing. The precious garden was watered so copiously with my small watering can, that Harry said I should drown the seeds, and Mama scolded me for getting myself so wet. There seemed nothing I could do but wait. At last a flush of green appeared. When, eventually, the multicoloured blossoms opened, I was entranced, swelling with pride when they were duly admired by the family.

Harry was the proud possessor of a bicycle. For a treat, he would put me on the saddle. With hands firmly grasping the handlebars, I was wheeled round the garden paths. I longed for the time to come when I should be old enough to ride a bicycle of my own. With my feet on the rests in front, the pedals whizzing around, I would coast down the hill, with the full sleeves of my blouse flapping delightfully in the wind. Each time I saw Miss Earp who lived nearby, perform this feat, I was lost in admiration.

Sometimes one of Harry's school mates Bill, who often came, would bring with him a penny farthing bicycle which had belonged to his father. In turn, the boys would mount the high seat and not always without mishap, meander round the garden, the small wheel wobbling incongruously after the big front one, to my great amusement.

After tea in winter, Harry played games with me till bedtime. Ludo and Tiddley Winks were great favourites. We sat at the table with its cosy red bobble edged cover. Stanley was in bed, Annie was studying; while Papa and Mama sat by the fire with the chess board between them, engrossed in their game. The big brass lamp which used to hang over the table, which could be raised or lowered on its chains, had been taken away. The room was now lit by gas burners. the jets in the sitting room covered by frail incandescent mantles. Sometimes these would become black, the light would dim, or in a sudden draught the mantles would fall to dust and have to be speedily replaced. In most of the rooms the blue and yellow naked flames of the gas jets flickered and hissed within their globes without the fragile mantles.

Sometimes Papa had to attend a meeting in the evening. Then Mama would busy herself with mending. By her side she placed two round wicker baskets. One was filled to the top with socks and stockings which needed darning. In the other were garments to be patched, or to have buttons and tapes renewed. The baskets never seemed to empty, in spite of Mama s industry. Each wash day provided a fresh supply. Linen buttons were bent, and others broken, while tapes became entangled and wrenched off by the heavy wooden rollers of the mangle.

We wore so many under garments all fastened by buttons or tapes, it was little wonder that the mending accumulated. Warmly wrapped in winter, I wore first a knitted woollen vest. Next, came the woven woollen combinations. Then, a sleeved buttoned bodice, with more buttons at the hem, to which were fastened my calico or flannelette drawers. Over these I wore a flannel petticoat tied with tapes at the waist; surmounting all these was a white petticoat fastened at the neck.

For Sundays and special occasions my flannel petticoat was not striped like the one for every day, but was of cream flannel, scalloped at the bottom and embroidered. Instead of calico, my best petticoat and drawers were made of fine nainsook, trimmed with Broderie Anglais. So with the addition of black woollen stockings I was successfully secured against the danger of cold air reaching any portion of my anatomy, except my face and hands.

# 2. Youth

WHEN MY SISTER Annie reached the age of sixteen, she became a pupil teacher in the British School. This tall forbidding building raised its head above the small houses which lay at the bottom of the hill on which our home stood. There were two departments in the school, one for girls, the other for infants. It was here that I was to start my schooling.

At first, I was full of excitement at the thought of going to school but as the day drew near I became uneasy. What happened in this new world that I was about to enter? Annie's hand was clutched very firmly by mine as we set out together. I had on my new 'pinny' and in my pocket was a rosy apple to eat at lunch time.

Annie took me through the playground into the school. When I found that my teacher was to be Edie Jackson, a pupil teacher friend of Annie's, much of my anxiety disappeared. As the big school bell began to ring, Annie left me, for she taught in the Girls' Department. In the playground the girls lined up according to their classes. Teacher showed me where to go, as they filed quietly into school. My seat was on the lowest tier of the gallery at one end of the room, with the other newcomers.

When we had sung a hymn and said the Lord's Prayer, we answered our names as they were called from the Register. Then I was given a small bag of coloured beads and a string on which to thread them. My eyes wandered round the strange new environment in which I found myself. There were three classes in the big room. The children in the middle class sat on forms, and those at the other end at long desks. On the opposite side of the room stood three easels with their blackboards; and in the middle was a large iron stove surrounded by a guard, with a very shiny top. Next to this was a desk with a high seat where a stern looking lady sat. This was Gov'ness. On the walls, were hung many pictures, some maps, and a long white roll of materials printed with short black words. This was used for singing lessons. As teacher pointed, we sang the Doh! Ray! Me! of the Tonic Sol Fah, following her voice.

When we listened to a story read by teacher, we sat with our arms folded behind our backs. One naughty little girl who was found to be eating sweets, had them taken away. She then had to sit with her hands clasped on her head as a punishment.

At playtime, I gave Elsie, another new little girl who sat next to me a bite of my apple. We stood by the wall and watched the others playing their noisy games. For some time we were too shy to join them, but when we did, what fun it was.

So often I had watched from the window at home as children played their merry games in the street. How I had longed to join them, but this Mama would never permit. Boys trolled their iron hoops, spun their tops, and played tip-cat on the curb. Girls skipped with the rope sometimes stretched right across the street. Then in turn they ran through the whirling rope, or skipped a few steps before rejoining the end of the line.

There was little traffic to disturb their games. Occasionally the Toot! Toot! of Mr Bates' motor car would be heard. It was one of the very few in the town. Quickly the children gathered up their playthings and scattered to the safety of the pavement. They watched with fascination as, seated aloft in his wonderful horseless carriage, with rubber horn tooting, the brass lamps gleaming, Mr Bates gradually vanished from sight in a cloud of dust. Play was then happily resumed, the infrequent horse drawn vehicles causing little interruption.

Now, in the playground, I was at last able to take part in some of this fun. Full of zest I joined in the many games, taking particular delight in the jingles and actions of the various ring games. When I was chosen to play 'Poor Mary who sat a weeping for her true love' I tried hard, but with little success, to squeeze out a few real tears.

For Stanley and me, something of interest was always happening in the Street outside our home. One of the first sounds we heard in the morning was the ringing of the muffin man's bell. He strode along vigorously ringing, as he balanced a tray on his head. In this were bread rolls fresh from the oven, covered with a thick cloth to keep them warm. We could seldom persuade Mama to buy any, for she made her own bread, but we were convinced that those in the covered tray were something special.

At the other end of the day, when it became dusk, the lamplighter came with his long pole which had a hook at the end. We loved to watch as he lit the tall gas lamp which stood near our house, at the corner of the Street. When he hooked the small chain at the top of the lamp a pool of light suddenly flared into the surrounding darkness.

Occasionally gipsies came with their brightly coloured horse drawn caravans. Stanley and I were a little afraid of them, and should we be outside when they came, we quickly scampered indoors. Many were the tales we had heard of children being stolen, and taken by the gipsies into far off lands. We often sang a jingle which ran:-

> My mother said, I never should
> Play with the gipsies in the wood.
> If I did . . .

Then followed a list of the dire consequences which would befall us if this advice was not heeded.

We wondered if the babies, which these gipsy women carried wrapped securely in their dark shawls, were stolen. The gipsy men seemed to us particularly sinister with their swarthy faces, black moustaches, large gold earrings dangling from their ears.

Another visitor to the Street we thought must surely have come straight from the land of faerie. He was tall and thin and wore a coat which reached to his heels. On his head he wore a red hat shaped like a plant pot. From it sprouted a thick black tassel. He walked in the middle of the road and pushed before him a strange contraption. As he pushed, he chanted a loud but rather melancholy theme which sounded to us like meer-mer-ansh-mink! Was it some strange incantation that he uttered? As he disappeared and the chanting became a mere thread of sound, we wondered if he had vanished into the unknown world from whence he came. When we were told that his cry was really 'Chairs and umbrellas to mend' we refused to accept such a mundane explanation.

Beggars, too, wandered along the Street from time to time. Ragged and unkempt, they lifted up their voices as they slowly meandered along. The noise they produced could certainly not be called singing. It was a slow long drawn out wail, and any words there might have been, were quite indistinguishable. Mama would give Stanley and me a penny each to throw to the 'poor souls' as she called them.

A more welcome visitor was the man with the barrel organ. We enjoyed the lively tunes he played, but best of all we liked to see Joey the small monkey, who was chained to the organ. He sat on the top and held out his little red cap for pennies. One day when Mama had allowed me to put a coin in his hat, I watched the monkey for a time, then, on a sudden impulse, I asked the man if I could turn the handle of the organ. He agreed, but the sounds I produced were oddly jerky and not at all like the usual music. When I returned to my watching Mama she did not look at all pleased but said quite sharply, 'Go and wash your hands at once, Edith.'

Sometimes we had music of a different kind, when the German Bands came. The men wore uniforms that were strange to us, so were most of their tunes. The ones we knew and liked best at that time were 'I'll be your Sweetheart' and 'Just like the Ivy'. Stanleys' favourite was 'The honeysuckle and the bee.' I could play all these with one finger on the piano, but Annie could play them beautifully with both hands.

She often played the accompaniments when friends came for a musical evening. Occasionally, I was allowed to stay up a little later than usual to listen. I liked to hear Papa sing 'My pretty Jane' best of all. He looked at Mama as he sang, and she looked very happy, with a half smile on her face.

I wondered if I should ever be able to play as well as Annie. On Wednesday each week I had a music lesson. For this I went to the house of Miss Kite. It was always with a sinking heart that I set off with my music case for this weekly ordeal; for ordeal it certainly was. Miss Kite was impatient and quick tempered. When my nervous fingers stumbled too often on the wrong notes, I received a sharp tap on the knuckles from a hard blue pencil. Sometimes when my new 'piece' had been insufficiently practised the blue pencil beat a veritable tatoo, until my knuckles were sore. When the lesson was over, and the door was shut behind me, I dissolved into tears and gave way to the relief of them, until I reached the gas lamp at the corner. Here, I dried my eyes, mopped my face, and removed all traces of tears before reaching home. I was afraid that I might receive a lecture about practising more diligently in lieu of sympathy; so Mama never knew how much I disliked my music lessons with the blue pencil accompaniment.

One Saturday afternoon I was practising my scales on the piano in the drawing room, when Stanley came in. I was glad of any distraction. Scales and exercises were forgotten and we began to play games. First, we tried to see who could swivel round for the longest time on the piano stool before the top parted from the base. Tiring of this, we decided to play at 'Circus.' Some weeks before, we had been taken to the Annual Fair and Circus which visited the town. The strident music of the merry-go-round with its galloping horses, gleaming brass and violent colours enchanted us. We were filled too with wonder and amazement at the sight of the animals and performers in the 'Big Top.' With this recent visit still fresh in our minds we began to set the scene.

From the ornaments upon the white marble mantelpiece, we made our selection. A pair of Marly horses stood at each end of the shelf. They reared up in a most dangerous fashion, with the riders tugging at the reins. These we thought, would do splendidly to lead the circus procession. They were placed in position and we looked to see what could follow. Vases we ignored, but we gleefully removed some little ebony elephants and put them in line behind the horses. Oh, joy! it was going to be a grand procession. Next we took down an alabaster bust of Queen Wilhelmina as a young girl. This had been given to Mama by a Dutch friend and was greatly prized. The charming little figure, we thought, could be our bare-backed rider and trapese artist, so she joined the others on the floor. What else could we use? My eye fell upon the lustres which still glittered on the mantelshelf. When they were shaken, or tapped lightly, their hanging chrystals gave a delicate fairy like sound. They would do for the band. We were just lifting them down carefully when Mama opened the door. She lifted her hands in horror 'Whatever are you children doing' she said. Sensing that a slap was imminent we quickly made our escape, leaving Mama to restore her treasures to their allotted places.

Each evening during the week Stanley and I were sponged down in front of the kitchen fire before being put to bed. But Friday was different for this was our real bath night. A large hip bath which was kept in the bathroom was brought downstairs for this occasion. It was blue with a projecting lip through which the water could be emptied. As it was not heavy we were given the exciting task of fetching it. Excitement there was, for it was no ordinary bath that came down the stairs. Under the spell of our childish magic it had been transformed into a sinister train—a 'cutting' train. As it slowly revolved on its downward journey its lip could cut into pieces anything which hindered its progress. To warn all and sundry its approach was heralded hy a loud Boom! Boom! This we produced by beating on the bottom of the bath chanting as we did so 'Make way for the cutting train. Boom! Boom! Make way for the cutting train.' In this way the perilous journey continued until the kitchen rug was reached. Then with one last Boom! the magic departed.

A delicious scent of cooking always lingered in the kitchen on bath nights for it was on Friday that Mama did her baking. After our bath we always had some special tit-bit instead of our usual biscuit. It might be a pastry-man with currants for eyes which Mama had made from 'spare' as she called her left over pastry. Sometimes it was a piece ot gingerbread, or a jam tart. First, however, the weekly ritual had to be performed, finger and toe nails were trimmed; my hair was carefully combed with a fine toothed comb—'Just in case'— Mama said. We were loth to leave the cosy atmosphere, and lingered as long as we could, but, at last, the cup of milk was drained, the last crumb eaten, and we knelt at Mama's knee to say our evening prayer. Later, when I was old enough to use the upstairs bathroom, I missed these cosy evenings and the excitement of the cutting train.

There was a great stir round and about at this time because of the approaching Diamond Jubilee of Queen Victoria. The streets were gay with flags and bunting and pictures of the Queen were everywhere. Many celebrations were planned. Some of the schools were uniting in a grand patriotic spectacle which was to be held in the Town Hall. The schoool which I attended was to produce a tableau representing the British Empire. I was very happy when chosen to take part as a Scottish girl. For this I was to wear a kilted skirt and shoes with buckles. The entertainment was to take place in the evening. This intensified my excitement, for it meant that I should really be able to stay up quite late, which was something I had longed to do. At last, I could experience the magic which always seemed to descend upon the world when I had gone to bed.

Early in the evening of the longed for day, the children who were taking part assembled in the school. I was thrilled with the colours ot the various costumes and highly delighted with my own. We were carefully scrutinised by Teacher, a few adjustments were made, and then we walked in a 'crocodile' to the nearby Town Hall. Here, we were shepherded into a side room to await our turn in the Programme. We were warned to keep very quiet and I found the waiting very dull. To amuse myself I wriggled my feet so that the light caught the shiny buckles on my shoes and made them twinkle. Tiring of this, I pretended to play a concertina by stretching and releasing the pleats of my plaid skirt. I didn't know then, what embarrassment the plaid would one day cause me. Waiting seemed endless and I became very drowsy. The subsequent happenings made little impact, the 'magic,' which I had so eagerly anticipated, completely eluded me.

The occasional parties to which we were invited were always a source of excited anticipation. When, one day, an invitation arrived for us to attend Billy Marshall's birthday party, this was especially the case. Billy had many treasures. In his garden he had some rabbits and a cage of doves. There were goldfish in his pool, but best of all was Belle, the friendly playful dog. We knew we should have a happy time at the party and were impatient for the day to come. For this special occasion we wore our Sunday clothes, Stanley his Eton suit, and I my new dress. This had been made from the plaid which I had worn at the Jubilee Celebration .

As there was more than enough material for the dress, Mama had made from the remainder a pair of drawers. I was not at all happy about these. They were quite an innovation, and like most children, I was very conservative about dress, disliking intensely anything which called attention to itself. When Mama said I was to wear the plaid ones to the party, I pleaded in vain to be allowed to wear my cotton drawers with the pretty frills, but Mama was adamant 'The plaid ones look very nice' she said, 'They were warm and comfortable' and, she added 'No one will see them.'

When we arrived, we found several other children there, all playing happily in the garden until tea time. Billy showed us the new baby rabbits and some of his other treasures. We then played ball games, in which Belle, with her tail furiously wagging, tried to join. At the bottom of the lawn was a swing and we decided to see who could go the highest by standing on the seat and working up. When my turn came, I worked away gaily, feeling happy and exhilarated. Belle was running round in circles barking joyously. as if she, too, were enjoying the party. Looking down, I could see the other boys and girls convulsed with merriment. What was amusing them? They were looking up and pointing. I, too, looked up, but could see nothing. The children's amusement continued as they still pointed. I again looked up. There was nothing to be seen. What could it be that they found so funny? Then the awful truth dawned on me. It was my plaid drawers at which they were laughing. They had seen white, pink flannelette, striped, and even red cotton ones, but plaid, never! I slowed down, and got off the swing. Not again, in the whole of my life, was I to feel so utterly deflated. To change from a soaring figure of ecstasy, to a figure of fun, was too sudden a transition. I was too proud to cry, but how I wished that I could suddenly disappear. My first impulse was to rush from the garden to the comfort of home, but I knew I could not go without Stanley, who would see no reason for leaving. The others were all now playing merrily together, quite unaware of the misery they had caused me. When eventually we went into tea, the delectable cakes, and other delicacies, helped to ease my wounded pride.

The outbreak of the Boer War made little impact on our childish minds. Certainly we played more often with our toy soldiers. From a tiny cannon we fired spent matches at the opposing army. Our commands were given in the loudest voices that we could muster, for we had heard the stentorian tones that were used when real soldiers in their gay scarlet tunics were on parade. As Papa was fond of martial music we were taken to hear some military bands. When Harry joined the volunteers we thought he looked quite resplendent in his new uniform but somehow strangely unfamiliar. Everywhere we went people were whistling or singing a new song which we quickly learnt:-
> Goodbye, Dolly I must leave you.
> Though it breaks my heart to go.
> Something tells me I am needed.
> At the Front to fight the foe.

We sang this as well as other popular ditties with no idea of their real import. War was something that was happening a long way off across the sea but of no real concern to us. More immediate problems exercised our minds. One of these was the forthcoming birthday of Mama. On what should we spend the precious pennies that we had saved? Choice was difficult but at last we decided on two plaques which we had greatly admired in a shop window. On one, in bright colours, was depicted the head and shoulders of Lord

Roberts, on the other was General French. When they were bought we waited with growing excitement for Mama to undo the parcel. At last she did so, the plaques were revealed in all their glory. Mama expressed her delight, kissed us and said we were very kind children.

We were secretly a little disappointed that our gifts were not given a place of honour in the drawing room or even the dining room, but Mama said she was sure we should enjoy looking at them. She found Lord Roberts a place on my bedroom mantelpiece, and one for General French on Stanley's.

# *3. Sundays*

SUNDAY ALWAYS BEGAN quite differently from the other days of the week. Instead of the jolly air that Papa usually whistled on his way to the bathroom in the morning, he whistled a hymn tune.

Breakfast was an hour later so I was glad when I was able to read, for the enforced quiet of that extra hour in bed, was less irksome. The baker's boy, with his tray of hot rolls, rang his bell in vain, as he passed our house. Nothing was ever bought on a Sunday, and only work that was really necessary was done. Lunch had been prepared the day before and consisted of casserole dishes, or ones that would simmer gently on the hob, and needed little attention. Janet, our little maid wore her black afternoon frock on Sunday morning, for there was little work to do. As soon as lunch was over, she had the rest of the day off.

There was little time after breakfast before we had to get ready for Church. All the family attended the Service and any visitor who happened to be staying also accompanied us. Our best clothes had been laid out ready. Mama helped Stanley to dress, but I was able to do almost everything for myself. Sometimes when I was trying to remove my 'pinny' the tape which tied it at the top would become knotted. My efforts to release it, made matters worse and Annie then came to the rescue. She also helped with the buttons on my shoes. I could not manage the buttonhook very well, and the buttons on my right hand glove I found difficult to fasten. When Stanley and I were ready we had to sit quietly and wait for the others.

At last we sallied forth, both clutching carefully the pennies which

Papa had given us for the collection. Mama wore her newest bonnet. The satin ribbons, which had been carefully ironed the previous day were tied in a crisp bow under her chin. When the weather was suitable she wore her mantle, a shoulder cape of rich black material, beaded and bugled, edged with lace. Stanley and I thought this was very beautiful. Mama held her long skirts bunched up carefully in her right hand to keep them from the dust or mire. The hem was protected at the edge with fuzzy braid. I longed for the day when I should be able to wear long skirts, and walk with them gracefully held up as Mama did. Many times I played at being a lady, by tying the sleeves of my coat round my waist so as to achieve the desired effect of a long skirt.

The Church we attended was about half a mile away from home, and was in the High Street. We could shorten the distance by using a lane which followed the old town wall. For me, this became a street of adventure. At the top of the high wall were several small dilapidated cottages. Each Sunday morning, as if awaiting our arrival, a horde ot unkempt children would be leaning over the wall, ready for any mischief. Papa was dressed in a frock coat and tall silk hat. This shiny target proved irresistible. With one accord the children up above tried to spit on it. How I hoped they would miss. Mama had brushed Papa's hat so lovingly, smoothing the nap carefully all one way, till it shone. What a pity if it should now be fouled. I never knew whether Papa was aware of this hazard. If so he gave no sign.

A little further along the lane was a small public house called the 'White Lion.' Over the door, on a bracket, was a plaster lion, fierce and menacing. Here we were near the end of our journey, for the High Street and Church were just round the corner. Nearby hung the Town clock, from which the chimes rang out with sonorous reverberation each hour of the day. My naughty brother, Harry, had told me that when the Town clock struck thirteen, the lion in the lane would leap to the ground and devour everyone in sight. Often, as we neared the dreaded beast, the clock would begin its deliberate preparation to strike the hour. How I hurried, and with what trepidation I listened, and counted, lest the fateful thirteen should be struck.

On my first visits to Church, when the congregation rose, and the singing began, I was filled with profound melancholy. The people did not appear to be ordinary every day men and women. I imagined that they spent their entire lives in this awe inspiring place, and my heart ached for them. The fact that they came out into the daylight when we did, made no difference. Maybe I had pored too long over the forbidding pictures of Dante's Inferno, in one of Papa's books that had a strange fascination for me.

This melancholy did not persist; I soon recognised the people that I knew. In a pew near ours, sat two sisters, the Misses Knollys. On the door of their house was a shiny brass plate, carrying the words MISSES KNOLLYS, COURT DRESSMAKERS. I wondered if they made dresses for the Queen. I knew they made beautiful ones for Mama. Annie greatly admired the Knolly sisters, and thought that they were very smart with their small waists. She had been told, she said, that their tiny waists were so tightly laced, that they had to undo their corsets before they could eat.

In front of us, in the next pew, sat Uncle James and Aunt Betsy. I amused myself during the sermon by watching Auntie and trying to emulate her mysterious movements. Aunt Betsy wore a bonnet on which were some feathery things which Mama said were Aigrettes. I used to watch with fascination as they quivered and shook. How clever she was to produce such a shaking, with no apparent movement of her head. Sunday after Sunday, I tried hard to make the flowers on my hat dance, and quiver in the same way but, according to Stanley, I had no success. We were more fortunate with another game which we often played to relieve the tedium. Across the aisle in a pew level with ours was a small boy whose name was Ronnie Bosher. He sat next to his father, who was on the outside seat. We had a similar place in our pew. First, we attracted Ronnie's attention. Then our game began. We peeped round Papa with only a small portion of our faces showing, and then withdrew in a kind of Peep Bo! Ronnie did the same. In a short time we leaned forward with more of our faces in view. Then, we showed our heads, and next, by edging forward in the seat, most of us could be seen. Ronnie followed each movement, but one Sunday the last effort proved his undoing and he overbalanced. As he fell, several hymn books were dislodged and accompanied him to the floor. There was considerable noise and confusion. We were very concerned so we sat back, to behave with the utmost decorum for the rest of the service.

Each Sunday afternoon Stanley and I went to Sunday School. One day when we were particularly early, we did what we considered to be a daring and even wicked thing. We thought that all shops were closed on Sunday, but in a nearby side street we had discovered one that kept open. It could hardly be called a shop, for it was really the front room of a small house. Here, toffee apples could be bought even on a Sunday. With considerable trepidation, lest we should be seen, or some unknown punishment overtake us, we entered the shop. For one halfpenny, we bought a toffee apple. We ate it between us, bite for bite. The apples were small and beneath the toffee coating, were also sour, but that mattered little against our sense of exciting naughtiness. We removed the traces from our hands and faces with our pocket handkerchiefs but, as we entered Sunday School, I had the uncomfortable feeling that Nemesis might descend at any moment, to chastise us for desecrating the Sabbath.

Sometimes there were occasions on which we visited the Church during the week. One of these was the wedding of Agnes, the only daughter of Uncle James and Aunt Betsy. Annie was bridesmaid, in a frock of blue silk with lots of frills. Her flower trimmed hat had blue ribbons hanging down at the back. With her blue eyes and long fair hair we thought she looked very pretty. I could hardly recognise the bride with her veil completely covering her face, the long white dress trailing behind her, but I thought what a lovely time we could have playing at 'Weddings' with myself, naturally, as the bride. Stanley was not enthusiastic over the idea until later when we had our photographs taken. The photographer kept popping under a black cloth and then telling us to smile while he counted three. Stanley thought that if we did play 'weddings' he would be the photographer.

Another occasion which had a profound effect upon me was the funeral of Mr Every. He was the owner of the works where Papa was manager. For some weeks Mr Every had been ill. Tan, which looked like wood chippings, had been strewn in the road before his house to deaden the sound of horses and wheels. Each day Papa made anxious enquiries, but at last the end came. We were all to attend the funeral, so Mama was very busy getting black clothes ready. Some new ones had to be bought, but not all, for most families had their funeral black ready for such occasions. It was the only fitting wear, whether the deceased was friend or relative. The time for which these funeral garments had to be worn was rigidly observed. Great lack of respect was shown if they were discarded too soon. Scorn was poured on any widow who gave up her widow's 'weeds' or was known to have attended any form of entertainment for at least a year after her bereavement.

On the death of the Queen, it was not only the Court that went into mourning, but most of the populace as well. Black was worn for some months, followed by mauve which was spoken of as 'half mourning.'

On the day of Mr Every's funeral we dressed in our sombre clothes and Mama gave us each a handkerchief with a black border. Taking our places in the waiting cab we joined the others which were assembling outside Mr Every's house. The widow was shrouded in black crepe, a veil of opaque material covered her face and hung to her waist in front, almost to her heels at the back. Black plumes waved in bunches above the heads of the coal black horses which drew the glass sided hearse. This, too, had black plumes at each corner.

The hearse took the longer way round to the Church. The houses on the way all had their blinds drawn, the shops, too, were shuttered, as a mark of respect. As the slow procession reached the entrance, the organist could be heard playing the 'Dead March in "Saul".' As I listened to the long drawn out Pom! Pom! Pom! melancholy overwhelmed me. The atmosphere seemed filled with gloom and dread, but it wasn't until the singing of 'Nearer, my God, to Thee,' that my profound misery found relief in tears which I was unable to stem.

I could not sleep that night. Between spasms of weeping, my thoughts were busy with the great imponderable. What was now happening to Mr Every? What did really happen when one died? On my bedroom wall hung a picture of 'The Heavenly Choir,' a group of winged cherubs. I wondered if all angels were young. Mr Every was old. Would he, too, have wings? From angels, my thoughts turned to fairies, and soon they became intermingled. Under their soothing influence, I fell into a fitful sleep.

A more joyful event occurred on the first Sunday in July each year. This was the anniversary of a small rural Chapel about six miles away from our town of Lewes. It was the custom for as many as possible of our congregation to join theirs for this celebration. The journey was made in a horse drawn brake. This was a high vehicle with bench like seats. On one occasion Stanley and I had the privilege of sitting in front with the driver. From this lofty perch we had a splendid uninterrupted view of the countryside. The grass verges of the road were gay with a tapestry of wild flowers. The bright yellow of the bedstraw and trefoil, mingled with the pink of rest harrow and the blue of ground ivy and bugle. Queen Anne's lace was everywhere, with here and there the arresting scarlet of the poppy. Hedges were spilling over with the creamy blossoms of the wild clematis, not yet seeded into the curly 'old Man's beard.' Sweet smelling honeysuckle was here too, intertwined with the delicate petals of the wild rose.

As we drove along we were very near the backs of the horses. Suddenly, the tail of one, Polly, rose, and she relieved herself, to the accompaniment of several loud reports. Our self control was taxed to the utmost, Stanley and I could hardly repress our giggles, but Mama was close behind. We knew that if we gave way to such unseemly behaviour it would bring a stern rebuke.

After the morning service at the Chapel we went to the village Inn for lunch. For us, this was a great novelty which we much enjoyed, especially as we had for 'afters' some delicious cherry pie. On the homeward journey in the evening, the Clop! Clop! of the horses' hooves almost lulled us into slumber, but we were not too sleepy to notice the white scuts of the many rabbits that frisked on the short turf of the hillside.

# 4. *Young Love*

As STANLEY AND I grew older with fresh interests coming into our lives we discarded many of our childish games. No longer did we resort to Mama's bedroom on rainy days, there to enact deeds of daring and fantasy. In this enchanted world a curtain could be transformed into the diaphanous dress of a fairy, or a shiny brass stair rod be changed by magic into the flashing sword Excalibur.

The magic had faded. Our histrionic efforts now became limited to the playing of Charades at Christmas.

When I became ten years old, Mama decided that I should leave the Pells school to become a pupil at Miss Smout's Seminary for Young Ladies. This seat of learning was in the High Street and comprised the top storey of a block of buildings. On the ground floor was a confectioners shop, among a group of offices.

My first few days in these new surroundings were strange and shy making. Miss Smout herself was somewhat forbidding. Her rigidly corseted figure was encased in a severe black frock, which fitted into her narrow waist without a wrinkle. A high collar encircled her neck, her leg of mutton sleeves full at the top, narrowed to a tight wrist band. To prevent any stray locks escaping, a thick net covered the large bun at the back of her head into which her abundant dark hair had been tightly coiled. Face and hands alone emerged rather starkly from her sombre garb. Miss Smout's only concession to ornamentation was a thin silver chain, which went round her neck and across her bodice to a small pocket, into which her watch, at the end of the chain, was tucked. Steel rimmed spectacles perched precariously on her long nose as she peered above them, with a severe expression.

The whole atmosphere of the school was far more subdued than that to which I was accustomed. There was no playground. Instead of noisy games with shrieks of uninhibited laughter, the girls chatted together in small groups.

During the lunch break the girls were allowed to visit the confectioner's shop below. Here, there was a most delicious assortment of cakes. Cream oozed from the éclairs, and from the fluffy cream buns which could be bought for twopence each. Such riotous spending was not for me. I contented myself with a lemon bun, topped with icing, at a cost of a halfpenny. The rest of my weekly pocket money of threepence, had to be conserved for sweets and other luxuries.

It was not long before I made friends with two of the girls who were sisters. Winifred, who was the same age as myself had many similar interests to my own. Olive, who was two years younger, was musical, and had a keen sense of fun. Soon we were spending as much as possible of our leisure time together, roaming the hills and woods in search of wild flowers. We found the haunts of the elusive bee orchid, the delicate blue round headed rampion, and the quaking grass, whose shiny brown fronds quivered perceptibly in the slightest breeze.

Often we climbed to the summit of a hill and sat on the cushions of aromatic wild thyme. Small blue butterflies fluttered around. Gorse bushes glowed with their riot of colour and bumble bees, drunk with honey, blundered from bloom to bloom. The drone of the bees and the trill of the larks which soared above us, were the only sounds except for an occasional Ting! Ting! Tong! from the small bells which hung round the necks of the free ranging sheep.

Sometimes we would amuse ourselves by rolly-pollying down the gentle slopes. Lying prone, we rolled over and over, gaining impetus with each yard, until we arrived at the bottom dishevelled but exhilarated. We tried to imagine what Miss Smout would think of such behaviour, and went into fits of laughter at the thought of Miss Smout herself rolly-pollying.

Sometimes Stanley came with us on our jaunts. Then we often took 'Tantivvy' our toboggan, which Harry had made and named for us. With yells of delight we skimmed at speed over the short slippery turf, toiling back to the very top of the hill after each excursion, so that not one yard of the ecstatic ride should be lost.

Winifred, Olive and I also learnt to swim, and what an arduous task it was. One of the few amenities of our small town was an open air swimming bath. The water, always intensely cold, came from the adjacent river. A high brick wall surrounded the bath to deter any peeping Tom. The sexes were severely segregated, special days being allotted to each. There was no instructor and seldom any attendant. We were left to our own devices but we helped each other when we could. To stop exercising, even for a short time, meant numb fingers and chattering teeth. When we emerged from the water, our voluminous striped cotton costumes hung heavily upon us, and we dithered with cold as we dressed in the unheated, cement floored, wooden cubicles.

On one evening in the week Stanley and I went to choir practice. Stanley was often chosen to sing solos, his favourites being 'Oh! for the wings of a dove' and 'Angels ever bright and fair.' His pure clear voice had an ethereal quality, and was much admired. Mama decided that he should have his voice properly trained and chose as his instructor Mr Teviot, who had a good reputation as an organist and choir master. He also gave piano lessons. With great relief, I was transferred from Miss Kite, with her dreaded blue pencil, to the kindly guidance of Mr Teviot. He was a gentle effeminate man with pale blue eyes, fair hair and a droopy moustache. A bachelor, he lived with his widowed mother in a small village called Barcombe, about three miles away from our little town of Lewes.

We had our singing lessons after school in the afternoon. As Mama usually invited Mr Teviot to take tea with us afterwards, we became quite friendly.

One summer it was arranged that we should spend part of our holiday at Mr Teviot's home at Barcombe. I was then thirteen and Stanley eleven. At first we were somewhat dubious about this. Former holidays had been spent at home, except when we all went with Papa and Mama for a week to the seaside. Now, at the thought of going to a strange place without the rest of the family, Stanley and I were a little uneasy.

Mr Teviot came for us and we travelled the few miles to Barcombe by train. From the station we had quite a long walk before we reached the village; Mrs Teviot was watching for us and she gave us each a kiss as we entered the cottage. She was a round dumpling of a woman with very rosy cheeks. 'Sit down, my dears' she said, 'and I will get you a glass of milk." We sat down shyly on the horsehair sofa under the window. As we waited, my eyes travelled round the small room. Behind us the windowsill was filled with raddled pots of scarlet geraniums. On the opposite side of the room was a piano. Standing on the cloth which covered the top, were many photographs, some in silver frames. A round table with a red chenille cover filled the centre of the room, and against the wall facing the fireplace was a chiffonier with glass panels in each of the cupboard doors. Among several vases and ornaments which graced the top was an oil lamp, on a thick woolly mat. By its side was a large leather bound book with a metal clasp. I could not tell whether it was a photo album or the family Bible.

Although it was summer, a fire burnt in the shiny blackleaded grate; brass fire irons twinkled in the hearth. A large black and white cat, whose name we later discovered was Tibby, was curled up cosily on the pegged rug before the fire.

When we had drunk our milk Mrs Teviot showed us our bedrooms. She opened a door near the fireplace and revealed a short flight of scrubbed uncarpeted stairs. At the top, on the right, was the bedroom that Stanley was to share with Mr Teviot. Passing through Mrs Teviot's bedroom on the left we came to a small slip of a room with whitewashed walls and a sloping ceiling. On the bed was a faded patchwork counterpane. The floor was scrubbed almost white like the stairs and by the side of the bed lay a pegged rug of many colours. A similar one was by the washstand. The jug and basin each had a bold pattern of crimson roses on a white ground. The chamber pot was similarly adorned. It sat flagrantly unconcealed on the shelf below. A few hooks on the door completed the furnishing. When we came downstairs a youth was talking to Mr Teviot. 'Hello Terry' said Mrs Teviot 'Meet my visitors, Edith and Stanley. You will be able to show them round.' This Terry seemed quite willing to do and we set off to explore the village. Next morning Terry arrived as soon as we had finished breakfast and each day was spent in the company of this entertaining and informative companion.

In the beech wood which climbed the hill behind the cottage, Terry pointed out the fox 'earths,' and the trail made by the night prowling badgers. He showed us the dreys of the many grey squirrels and the 'form' where a hare had sat concealed. We grew very fond of Terry, and I thought him most handsome with his blue eyes and fair wavy hair. Soon Terry and I walked hand in hand, and found Stanley's presence rather irksome. We tried now and again to hold a conversation in French so that he would not understand. Terry's vocabulary was far more extensive than mine, but when he wrote 'Je t'aime' on the top bar of a gate, I had no difficulty with the translation. On one particularly large beech bole in the wood many lover's initials were carved. When Terry one day carved thereon a heart surrounding the initials T, and E, for Terry and Edith, I was enraptured. Alas! the idyllic fortnight ended all too soon. Terry promised that he would drive over to see me the following Saturday with the small pony and tub in which he had taken us for several drives. We agreed on a meeting place, but it was with considerable misgiving on my part. What would mother say? This worried me, and exercised my mind all week. Finally, I came to the conclusion that she would disapprove so it would be better not to tell her. In this case, Terry must not come to the house. I decided that I would meet Terry at the appointed place and take him to 'The Pells' a beauty spot near home. Bess, the pony, could be tethered to one of the trees by the seats where we could sit and talk.

As Saturday approached I got more and more excited and anxious. Would Terry come? Would it rain? Would mother find me something to do that would prevent my going? Would Stanley want to come with me and give away my secret? How I wished to know the answer to all these worrying questions.

Saturday came at last. The sun shone, the sky was blue: I went through my allotted tasks in a dream. Stanley and I started out together. Our destination was supposedly the near-by newly opened playground, where there were swings and a see-saw. Happily for me, Stanley had decided to play cricket with some of his friends, in the field adjoining the playground. This left me free to meet Terry without any difficult explanation. When I arrived at the trysting place, he was already there. Bess, the pony, was contentedly nibbling at the grass verge. We soon made our way to 'The Pells,' where we sat for an hour that golden afternoon and discussed our future. Terry had not yet decided which career to choose. The choice for him lay between dentistry and engineering, and I listened with interest as he discussed each in turn. My profession had already been chosen. I was to follow in Annie's footsteps and become a teacher.

As we talked, the implication was that our future lives would be linked together. We parted, promising to meet again on the following Saturday and I went, full of 'Joie de vivre,' to collect Stanley before going home.

The next Saturday came with teeming rain and I knew there would be no meeting with Terry for another seven long days. As the days passed and the next weekend approached, my spirits rose. Saturday came at last and though the day was dull, it was fine, and I went gaily forth, for once, without Stanley. I reached the rendezvous, but there was no Terry. For a long time I waited, refusing to believe that he would not come. What had happened? I was sure that it wasn't Terry's fault, but how could I find out? Letters we had decided were unwise. Children's letters were never considered private, and parents reaction was unpredictable. I felt most dejected as I went slowly and sadly home to wait another week before the mystery could be solved.

Fate proved unkind, for during the week Aunty Emily wrote to say that she and Lucy, my favourite cousin, were coming for the day on Saturday. Lucy and I were the same age and I was generally delighted at the thought of a visit, but not this time. They arrived as promised, and in consequence we sat much longer over the mid-day meal, than was usual. When at last I did manage to set off with Lucy, it was much later than the time arranged for meeting Terry. He was not there, and my heart sank. Had he been and gone? I should never know, for when I went at the appointed time on the next Saturday there was no Terry. With a cold feeling of dismay, I felt that circumstances had been against us, and I sadly faced the fact that our idyll had ended.

I was glad that I had said nothing about Terry to Winifred. She and I spent a great deal of time together and had become good friends. We both went to School of Art for two evenings in the week. In the summer we swam, or went for long walks. In the winter we joined some evening classes for Physical Exercises, far more strenuous ones than Miss Smouts gentle ball throwing. Another evening of mine was taken up by piano and singing lessons, and there was choir practice each Friday. Time was fully occupied, a much quoted maxim being that 'Satan finds some mischief still for idle hands to do.' In addition to these activities, both Winifred and I were voracious readers. I had long outgrown the sympathy provoking, tear jerking and highly moral books of my childhood, such as 'Christy's old organ,' 'Blind Meg and her children' and the weepy 'Wide, wide world.' I had progressed through 'What Katy did at School' and

'Treasure Island.' Sometimes I changed the books at the Library for Mother and Harry. Often I read these before they did. On one occasion I overheard Harry say to Mother, 'I shouldn't let Edith read this one.' I smiled to myself, for I had already finished it, but I was greatly exercised as to what was in the book, that was unsuitable for my consumption, but I could find no clue.

We were all excited when we learnt that Cousin Tom was coming over from America to visit us. He had paid previous visits, but I had then been too young to remember him. When I saw him, I thought his clothes looked very odd, and Winifred said she wanted to giggle when she saw his spotted bow tie and peculiar hat but Tom proved to be a most entertaining companion. He accompanied Winifred, Olive and me on our walks and had a fund of amusing stories. With him, he had brought a number of songs, some humorous, some sentimental. These provided a pleasant variation when we had our sing-songs round the piano. We laughed heartily at his humorous ditties, which were new to us, and which he put over in great style. We each sang in turn except Mother, who would never sing solo but joined in when there was a chorus.

# 5. *The chosen career*

A S I APPROACHED my sixteenth birthday, I was faced with an examination, the result of which would determine whether or not I
could start my career as a teacher. If I failed the examination the
choice of any other occupation was strictly limited. Opportunities
for girls to earn their living were very few. Almost the only other
possibility for me was nursing. One day when Mother and I were in
Brighton, our nearest big town, Mother had taken me to a phrenolo-
gist. He 'read my bumps' carefully, feeling all over my cranium.
Then he announced his conclusion. Nursing he said was definitely
my vocation. I did not agree with him. The sight of suffering caused
me intense distress, and I had a most acute sense of smell. Neither of
these I felt were the attributes of an efficient nurse. What I should have
liked, had it been possible, was to earn my living by horticulture.
We knew of only two colleges devoted to this subject. At the one
fees were extremely high, the other, when approached, could give
no guarantee of a job when the training was completed. It would be
difficult for a female to compete in what had been purely a male
profession. So teaching it had to be, and the examination hurdle must
first be surmounted. Fortunately, I was successful, and it was with
mixed feelings that I said 'Goodbye' to Miss Smout and her Select
Seminary.

For the next two years I was to be both Pupil and Teacher. The
teaching was to be in my home town of Lewes, at Southover Infants'
School, and my academic studies in Brighton, at 'York Place,' there
being no suitable school in Lewes. This would mean travelling the

intervening eight miles by train. After the August holiday, I made my way one bright sunny morning to the Infants' School. Some small children accompanied by their mothers, were already filtering into the playground. I could feel curious eyes upon me, and knew that I should be the subject of speculation among the mothers at this school time gossip session. Miss Cade, the Headmistress, came forward to greet me. She was a middle aged spinster with greying hair swept away from her face and coiled in a neat bun at the nape of her neck. The severe black dress which she wore was relieved by a cream crocheted collar. On her nose were steel rimmed glasses. In spite of the severity of her looks, her manner was warm and friendly. Miss Cade then introduced me to her assistant teacher Miss Coles. She too was severely dressed, but appeared a little younger than Miss Cade. They both seemed rather old to me. Miss Coles was also a spinster, as practically no education authority in those days would employ a married woman. Little wonder that in the profession one found many unhappy, frustrated, and sometimes embittered women.

Southover School was small. There were only two classrooms, In the larger of these Miss Coles and I had our classes. A round bellied iron stove, surrounded by a strong metal fireguard, stood in the middle of the room. Small high windows were in each side wall. At one end of the room was a 'Gallery.' On tiers of wooden seats sat my class, the 'Babies.' Miss Coles children sat on forms attached to long ink stained desks, at the other end of the room, but there was little space between the classes. It was with a curious mixture of feelings that I first stood in front of those twenty Infants as 'Teacher.' Miss Coles and I were each addressed as 'Teacher.' Miss Cade was 'Gov'ness.'

The children were all unknown to me, and I felt that I must learn their names as soon as possible. This was not easy, for some of them were overcome by shyness when addressed. A few names were memorised by remembering that the brown curls belonged to Mary, the slight squint to Billy, and the freckles to Jane. The ages of the children in my class ranged from three years to five. The older ones were able to write their names on the slates with which they were provided. The slates were framed in wood and written upon by a slate pencil. Some of the pencils wrote fairly quietly, but some, if of harder slate, set one's teeth on edge with the shrill squeaks they produced. Each child brought to school a slate rag with which to clean the slate after use. Alas for hygiene! First, the slate was spat upon, and then rubbed with the rag. Unless frequently renewed, the sight and smell of the slate rags was distinctly unpleasant. When 'teacher' addressed the class or at story time, the order was first given 'Arms folded.' While they listened, the children sat with their arms either folded in front or behind their backs. Should one of them fidget or otherwise misbehave, the culprit had to sit with hands on head, so that all could see the one who had been naughty.

For the first few days the constant talking made my throat quite sore, as if scratched, but this gradually wore off. As the children became accustomed to me, I would often find a small hand stealing into mine during the playtime, and I was the recipient of many confidences. These were nearly all concerned with possessions 'I've got a baby brother,' 'We've got three kittens at our house' and so on. I enjoyed their childish prattle. Sometimes I was offered a gift of flowers, often wilting from being clutched too tightly in a small hot fist. These were always accorded a place of honour on my desk. I soon realised that I was enjoying my work, and felt sure that I had chosen the right vocation.

The term at the Brighton Centre began later than that of the Primary school, so it was not until mid-September that I caught the eight ten train one morning, to find my way there. I had been given explicit instructions how to reach it. The Centre was not far from the station, in a side street. I mounted the steps to the entrance, and rang the bell with some trepidation. The custodian, who answered the door directed me to the Head Master's room. I knocked timidly, and was told to enter. The Head, Mr Done, rose from his desk to greet me. He was a short stocky man, but gave an impression of power. His dark hair was thinning on top he was clean shaven, with an extremely well groomed look. Although he had a severe mien, I thought the lines that were etched near his eyes denoted humour. Mr Done first consulted a list on his desk then asked me various pertinent questions as to the schools I had attended, my hobbies, and so on. He concluded by saying 'You will be in Section C.' I found that 'C was the lowest grade, so I imagined that Mr Done had not formed a very high opinion of the erudition obtained at Miss Smout's Seminary.

For the first time I found myself in a mixed class, as half the scholars were boys; since my brief friendship with Terry, I had had no boy friend. There had been neither time nor opportunity to pro-mote a friendship with anyone but Winifred. One of the choir members would have liked to fill this role. He, Jimmy, had caused me some embarrassment by spending most of the time during the sermons, with his gaze fixed upon me. I had endured a certain amount of teasing because of this, and when it was discovered that he was writing poems, the teasing increased. One of his verses ran:—

'High up in the elm trees, the rooks are seen flying,
Bringing the sticks, to build up their old nest.
Would that I too, like the birds, could be trying,
To fashion a home for the one I love best.'

There were several more in the same strain and they were headed 'To Edith.'

Stanley was my chief tormentor. He sat next to Jimmy, and one day happening to get hold of one of Jimmy's effusions, he quoted and misquoted it to me in derision, whenever possible. No one suspected what a tease and torment this young brother of mine could be. He had a pure soprano voice, the notes soared effortlessly, with an ethereal quality but there was nothing ethereal about his teasing. Fortunately, I don't think Jimmy ever knew that he was the subject of fun. He was a handsome boy, with thick dark hair inclined to wave, and dark expressive eyes. Why he had no appeal for me, I shall never know.

I made friends with several of the girls at the Centre, especially with Isabelle Early, whose home was in Brighton. Isabelle and I sat together and often obtained identical marks in the exams. We were both in 'B' Section, to which I had soon been promoted, but I never attained the giddy heights of Section 'A'. Isabelle was a pretty girl, much more dress conscious than I. She confided that she was hoping to have a pair of shoes costing a guinea. I felt that they would be splendid indeed, for my best willow calf boots cost only sixteen and eleven pence.

We were just seventeen, at the age when it was customary to put up one's hair. This was a real landmark in the process of growing up. We decided to do it at the same time. Mine was fairly short and curly, tied back with ribbon. Isabelle's fair hair hung in a neat plait. We chose the day, and appeared together feeling very grown up. Isabelle's hair was now coiled in a neat bun at the back of her head, with a small velvet bow beneath it. Mine, I had gathered up to the top of my head, and tied with a bow of wide black sarsanet ribbon, three curls were brought forward and pinned, the bows then pulled out like a large black butterfly. It was a great occasion; we felt that we were the cynosure of all eyes. The boys were aware of the transformation and showed their approval, by smiles, and the raising of eyebrows.

It may have been because of the hair-do, that I now acquired a particular friend among the boys in my class. His name was Peter Polder. He sat behind me. I was first aware of his interest when he tweaked one of the small curls, which grew low on my neck. On the first occasion I ignored this, but its frequent repetition made it impossible to continue to do so. Turning, I gave him a hasty smile. After school, as I was on my way to the station, he was suddenly beside me. Peter was tall and broadshouldered, with brown hair and hazel eyes. I thought him very good looking. As we walked side by side he said 'You come from Lewes, don't you? I come from further up the line, but I could come your way round, so look out for me in the morning'. He scurried away to catch his train. As I waited for mine on the Brighton platform, my thoughts were full of Peter. Would he be at Lewes in the morning? How soon could I tell Winifred, and what would she say?

Next morning Peter was waiting for me. I could feel the blush rising to my cheeks as we met. He had to leave home ten minutes earlier to come via Lewes; the journey also necessitated a change of trains en route. This proved no deterrent, as Peter continued to travel this way with few exceptions. The train was always full of students and business men but we enjoyed the journey. From the station, he carried my books as well as his own, until we got within a hundred yards of the school. There we parted, for it was a strict rule that girls and boys should not be seen together within this limit.

One day we were granted a half holiday from Centre. Peter thought this would be a wonderful opportunity for us to spend the afternoon together as he need not go home until his usual time. Unfortunately, I had told mother that the holiday was expected, now I was afraid that this might complicate matters. Peter said he would come to Lewes after lunch, when I could show him round our little town. To this I agreed with some consternation which I hoped was not apparent. What would Mother say? Would she disapprove?

Unfortunately for me, Annie was at home. She was teaching at a school some thirty miles from home and, as a rule, only came at weekends. Her school, however, was closed for an epidemic. When the mid-day meal was over, I had still not ventured to mention my assignment with Peter. Judge of my dismay, when Mother suggested that, as Annie and I were both at home, we could help her to hang the new curtains, which had been made for the front windows of the house. Annie had persuaded Mother to replace the Nottingham lace curtains, which had been popular for many years, with curtains of cream casement cloth. This was quite an innovation, and Mother was eager to see the effect when they were hung. It might be a long job, with no afternoon left. The thought of Peter, kicking his heels impatiently at the station, spurred me on. I said 'Mother, I am sorry I can't help, because I've arranged to go for a walk this afternoon, with a friend from Centre.' 'Oh' said Mother, 'Which friend, Isabelle?' 'No' I replied 'Peter.' 'A boy' Mother's tone was faintly incredulous 'What is he like?' 'He is a very nice boy' I said 'I see him sometimes on the train. He comes from Three Bridges, and he is waiting at the station now.' Mother was silent for a moment. To my relief she said 'Well, you may go, but you must bring him home for me to see.' 'Oh yes' I murmured, as I flew to get my hat, and make my escape, before any more injunctions could be uttered.

Peter was waiting. When I had shown him the few things of interest in the town we started towards home. I liked, less and less, the idea of confronting him with Mother and Annie. We approached the house, but I did not even tell Peter it was my home we were passing. Straight on we went, past the ornamental lake, and on to the hills. The sun shone, the larks sang, and the corn rippled like the sea. By the edge of the field, the corn marigolds meandered like a length of yellow ribbon. Unable to resist gathering some, I interspersed them with gay poppies, corn cockles and the rather sparse corn-flowers. A bright but transient bouquet.

We sat for a while on top of the hill, with the gentle breeze fanning our faces. The land below stretched away to a blue horizon, the scent from the trodden thyme rose like incense around us. Soon it was time to leave, if Peter was to catch his usual train. We came down the hill hand in hand, with giant strides, ending with a slip and a slither at the bottom. I went to the station with Peter, and then returned home to face whatever was to come.

This one idyllic walk was the only one Peter and I ever took together. It was in fact, the only time that we were alone together, except for the few  moments between the station and Centre. Although we were not aware of it, this pleasant interlude was soon to end.

# 6. Departure

WINIFRED AND I, at this time had become deeply interested in Theology. Mr Preece, the superintendent of our Sunday School had studied various religions which he discussed with the older scholars. He read to us extracts from the Koran, and other religious works, and introduced us to Buddhism, by reading 'The Light of Asia.'

In turn, I discussed the information I had received with Winifred, who attended no Sunday School. She too, found the subject engrossing. I was fascinated, and wished to learn more. Mr Precee had a tailoring business in the High Street. Often, when sent on errands, I would call on Mr Preece who was always ready to talk on his favourite subject, the many systems of faith and worship in the world. Sitting on the counter, I listened enthralled, and took no count of time. This led to prohibition, for when I had returned home late on several occasions, I was never again sent to shop, without a monitory note from Mother 'Come straight back, and don't go to see Mr Preece.'

The visits would not have long continued. Mr Preece, alas! had no business acumen, and he became bankrupt. I remembered then the absence of customers, and the time he always had at his disposal. He left the town to live with a married daughter. I never saw him again, but often remembered with affection the kindly, wise instructor, who had opened for me such wide horizons.

I had been at Centre a year before Winifred was able to begin her studies there. We had both eagerly anticipated this, as it would mean that we should have much more time together. On the first morning that Winifred arrived to catch the train for Brighton, I introduced her to Peter, who was waiting as usual on the platform. Naturally we travelled together. As the days went on, Peter became strangely silent. I was at a loss to account for his displeasure and tried hard to restore the former happy atmosphere. One morning he was not waiting. As soon as I was in class, he surreptitiously passed me a note. This had no formal beginning but read curtly. 'You must choose between Winifred and me. If she comes, I shall not.' I was hurt and perplexed. How could I dismiss Winifred? We had to travel  on the same train. I could not possibly ask her to go in another carriage, or walk alone from the station to Centre. How very unkind it would be. We had been close friends for seven years, and I could not hurt her in this way—it was unthinkable. What a pity it would be if I had to lose Peter as a friend. I liked him so much and enjoyed his companionship, but we had not the community of tastes that existed between Winifred and myself.

I had always felt proud of my good looking boy friend, but, strangely enough, I had not regarded him as a sweetheart, in the way I had thought of Terry so many years before. Much studying and concentrating on a career seemed to have pushed the thought of matrimony into the background. That was for the future and might or might not happen. For one thing, I was abysmally ignorant. Any talk of sex was taboo. Mother had tried with embarrassment to impart a little lnowledge, but this had consisted mostly of warnings against familiarity with boys. The dire consequences that might follow, I assumed, would be the birth of an illegitimate baby —the ultimate disgrace. I was not the only girl at that time, incredible though it seems, who thought it possible for a male kiss to induce pregnancy.

Peter and I had walked hand in hand, but that was our nearest approach to intimacy. Naturally there had been no kissing. Had our relationship been a warmer one, I should no doubt have felt differently about parting from Peter. I might even have asked Winifred to suggest a compromise. As it was, my loyalty to her prevailed. Peter used the direct train route to Brighton again so the platform at Lewes knew him no more. Thereafter we avoided each other in class as much as we posisbly could.

Life moved along very pleasantly both at School and Centre. Towards the end of the second year, we began to be obsessed with the thought of the final exams. They were important, for on their results depended whether one could go to College or not. Places in the most favoured Colleges were not easy to obtain. If one's standard in the examination was not sufficiently high, College was out of the question. Without a College training the salary would be less, the status considerably lower. In fact, there was only one lower grade, that of the supplementary teacher, of whom it was said in derision, that the only qualifications required were, that the candidate should be eighteen and vaccinated. So, however negligent we had been, we now concentrated on study, to the exclusion of all else.

At last the ordeal was over, with sighs of relief we saw the last papers collected. The rest of the term was spent in the exchange of photos and addresses, with autograph albums being inscribed with suitable quotations, or ribald rhymes. Various pleasant activities were engaged in. One glorious day, all who could, joined in a ramble over the hills, organised by Mr Done, the Head. The weather was perfect. There was little wind, the sun shone, the sky was blue, the larks trilled unceasingly. We walked, talked, and sang part songs. sitting in groups we ate our picnic lunch. It was a very happy day, which left an ineffaceable memory.

Finally, there was the breaking up party. The entertainment provided by the pupils revealed many unsuspected talents. There were vocal and instrumental soloists of such ability, that one wondered how they had found time to achieve such a high standard. One insignificant looking youth proved himself to be a gifted cartoonist. With blackboard and chalk he presented the Staff as he saw them. One rotund mistress was instantly recognised, although portrayed completely in circles. A tall attenuated master was depicted by a series of angles. The highlight of the evening however, was a sketch given by the boys, or should I say, young men. In one episode they impersonated the Head, with all his many little mannerisms of speech and gesture. We were convulsed with laughter, and so, to our great joy was Mr Done himself. So far from resenting it, when he made his concluding speech, he complimented the producer on the excellent sketch.

It was a very jolly evening, but with a tinge of sadness, for it was the last time we should all be together; many of us would never meet again.

During the last week Mr Done had each of us individually into his office, to discuss our future plans, always taking it for granted that we had passed the exam. He spoke of the merits of the various Colleges we might enter, saying which he thought would be best in each particular case. For myself he suggested one in London. This delighted me, for the London ones required a very high standard and I assumed that this was what he expected from me. I was reminded of our first interview when he had allocated me to a lowly place in Section 'C'.

In farewell, he presented us each with a testimonial. I could hardly wait to see how he had assessed my potentiality as a teacher. When I did read what he had written, I was surprised and delighted, but hoped that I should be able to maintain the high qualities he had ascribed to me.

So ended the happy years as a pupil teacher. After the summer vacation, a new vista would open, another turning in life's highway.

During the holidays, the examination result came and exceeded my expectation, for I had managed to collect a distinction in three subjects. This was most gratifying, as I knew now that it might be possible for me to attend the College of Mr Done's choice. Application was duly made, enclosing the testimonial from Centre, and I was accepted.

A list of requirements was furnished by the College, and a very extensive one it was. Material had to be bought, and an orgy of sewing was begun. Annie was home for the school holiday, and though somewhat unwilling was persuaded to help. She liked cutting out, so this was her task; she had little patience with fine sewing. Mother did the machining, while I did the finishing off and the sewing on of the innumerable name tapes. A new large trunk had been purchased and into this were piled the completed garments.

At last, the long job was finished, for the rest of the holiday I was free to spend my leisure as I pleased. Winifred, Olive and I went for long walks over the hills, sometimes taking a picnic lunch and spending most of the day 'far from the madding crowd,' our only companions, the grazing sheep: the sigh of the wind, with the song of the birds, our only music. We also swam whenever possible, in spite of the icy water in the Baths, fortifying ourselves after the swim by consuming sugar topped biscuits which we bought for fourpence a pound.

The holidays seemed to pass at incredible speed. Surely no days had ever before sped at such a rate. There were so many things we wished to do. Our old haunts were revisited, our youthful escapades remembered. I had an underlying feeling that things would never be the same again. The carefree garment of youth would be shed, as responsibilities mounted. Blossoms must inevitably fall if fruit is to form. So we made the most of these last days of freedom.

When the schools reassembled, I visited Southover to say Farewell! to the scholars and staff. There was a warm welcome for me, and I realised how fortunate I had been, that my first efforts at teaching had taken place in such a happy environment.

Other visits were paid and 'Farewells' said, their sadness being tempered by the bubble of excitement which kept welling up, at the thought of the adventure before me. At last the day of departure arrived: last minute chores were done. My railway ticket and some 'change' for tips on the way, were in my purse which was tucked into my right hand coat pocket with my handkerchief pushed on top to keep it secure. A golden sovereign for pocket money was carefully pinned inside an inner pocket. my sandwiches, too, were stowed away. Now the trunk, labelled and corded, stood ready. In spite of my excitement I was somewhat perturbed at the thought of taking the journey alone but father was at business, Annie and my elder brother were away fom home, Stanley was at school. When the cab came to take me and my luggage to the station, Mother with tears in her eyes said 'Goodbye' to me before I left the house. Partings always upset her and she preferred that her emotion should not be revealed in public.

# 7. College

I HAD BEEN to London on several occasions. With the family I had visited Art Galleries as well as various other Exhibitions, including the 'White City,' but I had never had to find my own way. However, by what I discovered later, to be a very devious route, I arrived at the College. It was an imposing building standing in extensive grounds, well laid out with lawns and shrubberies. I noted some beautiful trees, a large magnolia, also a tulip tree among them, as the cabby drove me to the main entrance.

Here, I was received by a charming girl, who seemed to me very soigné and adult. She was, I discovered, the head girl. Having greeted me, she passed me to another senior student who was to be my College Mother who would initiate me into College ways. I was shown to my bed sitter, a cubicle whose wooden partitions reached but a short way to the lofty ceiling. There was no door, but a brightly striped curtain hung at the entrance. The room contained a single bed, with a minimum of other furniture. The floor was bare, but Mary showed me a storeroom, where there were numerous rugs that could be used. As I had arrived later than most, these had been well picked over, the assortment that was left, had seen better days. We found one or two with which we were able to cover the bare floor.

There were eight cubicles in the dormitory to which I had been assigned. Most of these had a window. Mine however, had no window, but its place was taken by a large open fireplace. The disadvantage of this I was to discover later, when I found that it was the only source of heat for the whole dormitory. When the weather became cold, the fire was lit, and after 'lights out' the girls would all crowd into my room for a warm. They sat on the bed, and on the floor. It was jolly and cosy. We talked in hushed whispers, lest the sound should reach the ears of the Dorm' Mistress in her room at the end. Visiting at this late hour was strictly prohibited. How stuffy the room was when they had gone. I thought longingly of my bedroom at home, with its two windows, which opened to the sweet air of the hills.

The Principal and Vice-Principal of the College were both men. The rest of the Staff was composed of women. The Principal, big and pompous, taught divinity, the V.P. as we called the Vice-Principal, was responsible for music; a splendid and versatile musician, his lessons were sheer joy. My first encounter with him was when he tried the voices of the newcomers. Seated at the piano, he played the opening bars of an unfamilar hymn, and said 'Sing this please, in Tonic-Sol-Fa.' I tried, but it was years since I had sung in this way, and I made a poor attempt.
'Could I please sing the words?' I asked
'Oh yes if you can' he replied.
This I managed to do. He was evidently pleased, for he said 'I should like you in the choir.' His decision delighted me. That evening I joined the other choristers in the Gallery, at the back of the College Chapel. Besides choir practise our syllabus contained many music sessions for which students were divided into groups. I not only attended the group, to which I was allotted, but also any of the others, when the opportunity occurred. These were a source of the utmost pleasure to me under the tuition of the gifted V.P.

Another musical highlight was the annual performance of a Gilbert & Sullivan Opera. The senior students entertained us with the 'Mikado' and our contribution, for the first year, was to be the 'Gondoliers.' I was cast as 'Guiseppe.' When, in rehearsal, I raised a laugh by tweaking the cape of the 'Duke of Plaza Toro' I was severely reprimanded by the V.P. Until now, I had little acquaintance with 'Gilbert and Sullivan.' Our little town had not provided much entertainment of any kind. The 'Messiah' was performed annually by a mixed choir in the Town Hall. In this I had participated, but musically, there was little else of note. Of course I had heard many of the solos from the operas, sung at various concerts, but I had never seen a whole opera performed. It was a surprise to me when I found how seriously these works of Gilbert & Sullivan were regarded.

From the V.P. I learnt that they were a tradition, and no frivolous by-play could possibly be allowed. I was duly repentant and promised that, in future, I would not depart from the conventional observance.

Winifred, of course, was still at Centre. I missed her companionship, but I soon made friends with some of the girls, particularly with Penny Hamlett, one of the seniors. A Londoner, she introduced me to many facets of life, of which I was ignorant, warning me of the dangers which lurked in a big City for unsuspecting maidens.

Her Mother, she told me, was a spiritualist. Of this cult, I had no knowledge, so I listened avidly as Penny discoursed thereon. One evening she asked me if I would like to take part in a séance with her. I eagerly agreed. She was not very good, she said, but would do what she could. Her method of communication would be by knocking. I followed her to her room in excited anticipation, full of curiosity, but also with a little trepidation.

Penny made preparation, and the séance began. She was the lone performer. I sat mute, watched, and listened. Penny asked questions and interpreted the answers, by the various knockings which followed. Much of it left little impression on me. One thing however stayed in my memory, to be recalled many years later. This was to the effect that I had a spirit guide, whose name was Miriam.

I was very sorry when Penny left, a year before my course was finished. It was not long before she wrote to say that she had a beau. I was not at all surprised, for not only was she attractive but also a most entertaining companion. This was in direct contrast to another student, Priggy, who began to pester me with her attentions. Priggy, as she had been nick-named, was very clever. Exams she took in her stride, obtaining distinctions in almost every subject. While the rest of us bothered our brains with a lot of irrelevant detail, Priggy seemed able to pick out the salient facts and concentrate only on them.

At this time Stanley, my brother, was taking his exams. He had failed once, and was very anxious that his second effort should succeed. History which I adored, was his weakest subject. He wrote to me, asking if I would suggest what he should 'swot' for the forthcoming exam.

I showed the letter to Priggy, and without consulting any text book, she said 'Oh, this, and this, and this' and she gave me six items which she thought might appear in the exam-paper. How right she was. To Stanley's delight, four out of the six did appear and this time he was successful. This ability seemed to be Priggy's only gift, for of social graces she had none, and she was most unpopular. Priggy conceived a great affection for me, which I considered a nuisance. Many of the girls had a similar feeling for some of the younger mistresses, being 'smut' we called it.

I suppose it was inevitable. With only female companionship, when normally, those who were marriage ripe, would have found a mate, some outlet had to be found for their pent up feelings. With Priggy, this took the form of showering me with attention. She kept my cubicle scrupulously tidy with sometimes an offering of flowers. I was sorry that I could not feel the affection for her that I felt for May, another of my class-mates. May shared a dual task with me. She was a tall slim gentle girl, quiet but with a great sense of humour. In class we were arranged alphabetically. May and I had very similar sur-names. As we were always addressed as Miss So and So this similarity caused great confusion to one of the younger mistresses. She appeared little older than some of the students so it was perhaps not surprising that she seemed somewhat diffident and easily embarrassed. May and I derived a great deal of amusement by adding to her confusion over our names. When asked for her note book May would substitute mine and vice versa. It seemed very funny to us at the time. We little knew then, how we were to suffer in later years when our own pupils discovered our little weaknesses and played upon them.

The food at College was dull, and unappetising. The menu was always the same each week. We knew that the lunch we had on the first Monday of the term, would be exactly the same as the one we had on the last Monday. We had derogatory names for most of the dishes. The Friday steamed cod, with its dreary white sauce was 'Whale and white wash.' After Mother's succulent dishes, I found the food dis-tasteful, and my robust appetite vanished. As a consequence of the poor food, the polluted air, and, in the winter, the yellow pea soup fog which seeped in everywhere, the girls suffered from many minor ailments. One which afflicted me was a painful whitlow on my left thumb, which left me with a permanently corrugated nail.

So many girls were dissatisfied with the food, that they called a meeting, at which a deputation was chosen to lay our complaint be-fore the Head. This was received with great indignation by the Princi-pal. In a blustering, overbearing manner, he assured them that the food was the best that could be bought, the cooks were most efficient, so nothing could be improved. As to monotony, this he said, made for speed and efficiency.

One good thing, however, emerged as a result of the interview. He announced one day, that a gas ring was being fitted at one end of the Gym. With this, the girls could make themselves tea or any hot drink they wished. We already supplemented our diet by buying marmalade, jam and cakes, but we welcomed the idea of being able to have a 'cuppa' at odd times. We soon discovered a snag. It was a puzzle as to where, and how, we could obtain any milk. We had no contact with the visiting milkman. The nearest dairy was some distance from the College. To sally forth bearing a jug we felt would be infra. dig. The convenient milk bottles were not yet in use.

A bright idea struck me. Each morning I took an empty marmalade jar into the Dining Hall with me, and emerged with it half full of milk. At break, May and I thoroughly enjoyed our cups of milky cocoa, with biscuits which were always lavishly supplied by the College.

Unfortunately, our bright idea was soon copied. To the amazement of the housekeeper the milk consumption suddenly soared. This conundrum was puzzled over for a long time, till Miss Hoby, the housekeeper, thought of a possible solution. As we emerged from breakfast, one unfortunate morning, Miss Hoby was waiting for us. Tapping the girl who preceded me, on the shoulder, Miss Hoby said 'May I please look in your jar?' What luck! the scrutiny only revealed marmalade. She passed over my jar, with the purloined milk, but she found enough culprits to prove that her surmise was correct.

Thereafter, our milk at table was strictly rationed, so our odd drinks were either milkless, or made with the tinned variety. With pocket money already depleted by the purchase of a kettle, saucepan, tea and cocoa, as we had to buy milk, we had fewer drinks.

When at last Winifred joined me at College, our free time was soon fully occupied. There was so much we wanted to do, and see, in this wonderful City, that was of interest to us both. The only deterrent was our lack of funds. By the end of term, we were completely 'broke'. We carried our own luggage, when we went home, for we had no money left with which to tip a porter. I had a curious independence which forbade my writing home for more, although I knew that Stanley often had his pocket money supplemented.

Fortunately, it was possible to obtain a lot of pleasure for very little money. For fourpence by tram and underground, we could get to the West End, on our free Saturday afternoons. Here, we made straight to the theatre of our choice, and joined the crowd round the entrance to the Gallery. For one shilling we could climb the many steps to the 'Gods' and jostle our way to the best seats available. Was there discomfort? We never noticed it, when we could be captivated by such actors as H. B. Irving in 'The Bells,' Beerbohm Tree as 'Malvolio' and Julia Nielson & Fred Terry in 'The Scarlet Pimpernel'.

Sometimes, from our great height, the effect was apt to destroy the illusion, as when we could see the modicum of soil over which the grave-digger in 'Hamlet' was making such strenuous efforts, but for the most part, we were enthralled. No refreshments were provided in the interval, but we nibbled our penny bars of chocolate cream, with great content, surrounded by the aroma of oranges being eaten by some of the Gallery audience.

Descending to the street, the world of reality, we made our way to the nearest 'Lyons' for a hasty cup of tea and a bun. Then, back to College, our funds depleted by exactly half-a-crown.

The sporty girls had spent the afternoon playing tennis or hockey according to the season. Winifred and I both enjoyed tennis, but were not sufficiently expert to play in the matches. All students attended the Saturday evening choir practice, which took the place of the usual service. Most of us had spent a full, pleasant, and often strenuous afternoon. Some of us were somnolent, some over-tired. Often, on these Saturday evenings one of the girls would collapse in a faint; strangely this would trigger off a whole epidemic of fainting. Girls would flop, left, right and centre. I looked on in amazement. Surely so many attacks could not be genuine. Were they self-induced? Was it hysteria? It was hard to tell, but the spectacle repeated itself on many occasions.

Priggy was not at all pleased at the advent of Winifred. Her attentions redoubled. Poor Priggy! She was absolutely devoid of humour, completely rigid, with no compromise. Her sense of duty was overpowering. As Head Prefect, her discipline was exacting. Little escaped her vigilant eye, the slightest misdemeanour was instantly reported—a habit which endeared her to no one.

On one occasion Priggy did not appear for her usual duties. As she was absent also the following day, I asked if anyone knew the reason. No one did. I was somewhat worried and felt sure that I must find out at the first opportunity. There was no time during the day, the evening, too, was taken up by a rehearsal. It was not until I was getting into bed, that I remembered Priggy. Although it was for-bidden to leave the Dorm' at this late hour, I put on my dressing gown, and set off for Priggy's room, which was quite a distance from my own, but in the same block. This proved to be quite an eerie journey, with the dim lights and no sound but the plonk! plonk! of a dripping tap, from one of the bathrooms.

I reached her cubicle, and entered quietly, saying softly as I did so 'It's only me.' Priggy was awake. 'Hello' I said, 'What's wrong?' 'Why weren't you in class?' Learning that she had only had a bilious attack, and was now better, I left her, to retrace my steps. Next morning I was summoned before the Mistress in charge of Priggy's Dorm'.

'I have been informed' she said 'By Miss Pearson, that you were in her dormitory last night after hours.'

'Yes Miss Miles,' I replied 'I was.'

'May I ask why you were there.'

I told her the reason. She was a pleasant understanding mistress, a great favourite. With a smile she said 'As you have been reported, I had to take up the matter. As you probably know, Miss Pearson has an overwhelming sense of duty. She felt bound to bring to my notice, an infringement of the rules. Please observe them in future.' Still smiling she dismissed me.


Since Cousin Tom's last visit to England, we had corresponded frequently, and he had sent me numerous gifts. They were mostly of music, principally songs, sentimental and humorous. Among them were 'The Rosary,' and the 'Indian Love Lyrics.' One day I had a letter from him telling me that he was about to pay one of his periodic visits to England and the Continent. He had an inventive brain; his visit concerned the patenting of one of his inventions. Knowing that we had an occasional free week-end, he said that if I would let him know when this would be, he would arrange to be in London and would take me to a show on the Saturday. I could hardly wait to tell Winifred the exciting news, I considered asking if she could come with us, but decided against it.

The looked for week-end came at last, and Tom arrived at College to meet me. He had booked, he said, for 'Our Miss Gibbs,' a musical, so we went straight to the theatre. As usual, he proved a most entertaining companion. I was enjoying myself immensely, until the interval, when to my extreme surprise, Tom asked if I would marry him. I wondered if this was a sudden impulse on his part. Our frequent letters had been full of affection, but nothing in his had prepared me for this. Marriage, was still, to my mind, on the far horizon. I was very fond of Tom, greatly enjoyed his company, but had always unconsciously regarded him as a jolly, generous, elder brother, so I had never thought of him as a suitor. Taken unawares, I was confused, and could only stammer out my regrets. I did manage to say that I had not yet finished my training, all would be wasted if it were not put into practice. Tom brushed this aside, as he told me of the advantages of life in America. The picture he painted was a rosy one. We could travel he said, and see the world together. This was certainly alluring, but it was really at marriage itself that I baulked. I was too ignorant, and still regarded the state of matrimony as mysterious and certainly indecorous, according to my puritan upbringing.

How could I explain all this to Tom? It was quite beyond me. Tom was puzzled by my hesitation. 'Is there somebody else' he asked. 'Oh no' I hastened to reply. 'Well, then' he said, 'Suppose you think it over, and give me my answer when I return from the Continent.' 'It will still be "No" Tom' I murmured in confusion. 'Suppose we leave it for the present' he said, as we returned to the play. What happened to 'Our Miss Gibbs' after the interval, I do not think either Tom, nor I, knew, or cared. He took me back to College, and we parted with our usual cousinly 'peck.'

Suddenly I realised that I was hungry. Tom had bought me some chocolates in the theatre, but had not offered to take me for a meal afterwards. My mind, and possibly his, had been too disturbed, to think of such an obvious thing.

Tea time was over at College and everywhere was quiet. I made myself some milkless tea in the dreary Gym' and found some left over biscuits, soft and unappetising. From the cheerful anticipation of the morning, my mood had become as dull and depressing as the soggy biscuits, which I ate with distaste.

# 8. Rural joys

COLLEGE DAYS ENDED with the usual exchange of photos, addresses, and promises to keep in touch. The chief problem for each of us when we had left, was to find a job as teacher. There were far more applicants than there were vacancies. Some of the students who had left College the previous year were still seeking regular work, so the problem was acute. Eagerly I scanned the teaching periodicals for the few vacancies that were advertised. I answered several without result, so I felt relief and gratitude when I was offered a temporary post at the Infant School in which I had been a Pupil teacher. As it was to be only temporary, my search went on, and was at last rewarded. I was invited for an interview to a country school in Hampshire.

On a bright Spring morning, I set out to keep the appointment. The Vicar of the Parish, who was Chairman, and also Correspondent of the School Committee, had written to say that I should be met at Basingstoke, the nearest railway station. Met I was, by a ruddy faced countryman, in breeches and shiny leggings. He was a man of few words, and had little to say, as we bowled along the seven miles to Tadley, in his high trap.

From my lofty perch. I had a good view of the surrounding country, and could see woods, and stretches of common. The soil appeared light and sandy, which promised a new and happy hunting ground for wild flowers, should my application prove successful.

We drove to the Vicarage, which stood at the end of a long drive. Daffodils in the borders, were in full bloom and stood jaunty and gay in the sunshine. The Vicar met me at the door, and, apologising for the absence of his wife, suggested that I might like a wash after my long journey.

He then accompanied me to the meeting, which was held in the Parish room. This adjoined the Church, which, with the School and the Vicarage, formed the nucleus of the Village.

There were four men on the Committee besides the Vicar. One was a big burly man, with a rubicund face. Next to him sat my un-communicative driver, who gave me a fleeting smile. Of the other two, one, was an attenuated, but distinguished looking man, who appeared to be deaf, for he sat with his ear cupped in his hand. The last member of the Group, was a phlegmatic individual, who regarded me with an owl-like gaze through his heavily rimmed glasses.

Having introduced me, the Vicar began by saying, 'Well! gentlemen you have all read the testimonials. Now that the candidate is here, are there any questions you would like to put to her?'
There was silence, broken at last by the burly member who said with a broad accent.
'How do you think you would like to live in Tadley, Miss?' 'Would you like it here?'
I replied suitably. The next question came from the thin man. He wanted to know if I thought I could teach older children, as most of my experience seemed to have been among the younger ones. When I assured them on this point, there were a few more questions which were not particularly pertinent. I was then asked to retire, into what was evidently the kitchen, while they held a consultation. The meeting ended with hand shakes all round, but I was not informed of their decision.

However, on the way back to the Vicarage, the Vicar told me that they had been unanimous in deciding that I should be appointed. This would be conveyed to me in writing, but he thought I would like to know at once. Naturally, I was delighted. The salary, I knew would be £72 a year. This was not the best paying County, but I was quite happy at securing a permanent position.

When we reached the Vicarage, the Vicar took me to the Dining Room, where a substantial tea was laid. Betty, the maid, brought in the tea pot, and also a jug of cocoa, which the Vicar said he thought I might prefer, to fortify me for the journey home. As time was running short, and the trap would soon be coming, he would leave me, so that I could make a good meal.

Soon, indeed, I heard the Clop! Clop! of the returning horse.

As I said 'Goodbye,' the Vicar gave me a large bunch of daffodils. I thought that if the rest of the villagers proved as kind and thoughtful as he, I was set for a very happy time.

When I arrived to take up my duties, I met the Headmaster for the first time. He had not been at the Managers' Meeting when I was appointed, as he was suffering from a severe attack of 'Flu. The school was a small one, with about seventy scholars. Mr Barrett and his wife both taught there. I was the only other assistant. Mrs Barrett had the infants in one room, Mr Barrett and I taught the rest, in a larger classroom. The Barretts had found me some 'Digs' in a small farmhouse, some distance from the school.

My pupils were a great contrast to those I had taught before. I found the broad dialect of some of the children quite difficult to understand. Not far from the school was a more or less permanent gipsy encampment, from which some of the children attended the school sporadically. The ages of the pupils in my class should have ranged from seven, to ten, or eleven, but as some of the gipsy children were behind with their learning, they stayed in my class, instead of being transferred, until the age of twelve or even fourteen. One of these was Elijah. All these particular gipsies had biblical names. Elijah was old for his years. and his behaviour often proved embarrassing.

When we played ring games Elijah would always manoeuvre so as to be next to me. He would squeeze my hand, in a meaningful way. When the game was 'two's and three's, he would manage to get behind me, clasping and pressing my waist. When it was no longer possible to ignore his attentions, I mentioned my problem to Mr Barrett, and Elijah was transferred to the Headmaster's class forthwith.

I was soon having a very happy time socially, being invited to private parties, and to all the Village functions. The Barretts kept open house for me. They were childless, and treated me with the interest, and consideration they might have given to a daughter. I joined the Church choir, and was also a frequent visitor to the Vicarage, where I often played croquet with Mr Tweedie, the Curate. He helped the Vicar in the administration of the two Churches, with their far flung parishes, for which he was responsible.

Mr Tweedie had recently come to the village, from the town and knew little of country customs and parlance. On one occasion when reading the lesson in Church, he convulsed the congregation by his pronunciation of 'an e-wee lamb', a faux pas which he never lived down.

Among the people that I met frequently at the Barretts, was a young man, Ernest Wood. He was the son of a neighbouring schoolmaster and was himself training to become a teacher. He was very musical, playing 'cello, piano and organ. As he was the only child, his mother doted on Ernest, and her attention often proved most irksome to him. On one occasion when he was offered wine at the Barretts, he accepted, but his mother piped up:—

'Only half a glass, Ernest, only half a glass.' Could anything be more calculated to make him lose face? in front of a girl too.

Ernest and I were thrown together a good deal. Mrs Barrett was very fond of Ernest, and she encouraged the friendship. As I now had my bicycle with me, we took long rides together. During them, I found, as I had expected, many wild flowers that were new to me. On the boggy common, cotton grass and sun dew abounded, the sweet butterfly orchids filled the air with perfume. In the hedges grew the lovely yellow burnet rose, and, for the first time, I saw in a clearing, a profusion of rose bay willow herb. Its startling colour entranced me. I little knew what a pernicious weed it was to become. Autumn brought a feast of colour. Maples glowed in the hedgerows, wild cherries highlighted the russet woods with crimson splendour.

The winter months were enlivened by many parties, Whist Drives, socials and dances. What fun these village festivities were. The dances were really a romp. We danced Polkas, Quadrilles, Waltzes, and most popular of all, the Lancers. The highlight of the Lancers was at the point when the men formed a ring, and swung the ladies off their feet, to the accompaniment of uninhibited shrieks of laughter. Rivulets of sweat chased each other down the faces of the men. They often brought a spare collar with them, for which the damp crumpled one was exchanged during the interval. White cotton gloves were worn to prevent sticky hands from soiling the ladies' dresses.

The ladies' faces did not show the result of their exertions to quite the same extent as those of the men. Face powder, which had only recently come into use, was a great help. It had to be used with discretion, for the powder was almost white. The subtle gradations of shade came later. Neither rouge nor lipstick was used. To paint one's face would have branded one as a loose woman.

In the interval, the only beverages served were tea and coffee.

If there happened to be a pub in the vicinity, the men who needed something stronger, would pop out to 'have one.' 'Nice' women never went into a public house. To have done so would have ruined one's reputation. Nor did women smoke in public. I had seen only one woman smoking outside the home. She was in a railway carriage, and was an American.

Refreshments at the dances were always home made. There were sausage rolls and meat patties, mince pies and lardy cakes, jam tarts, and a variety of smaller fancy cakes, many of them oozing with fresh cream. The music was played on a piano, sometimes accompanied by a violin. Ernest was often the pianist, and he would walk home with me afterwards.

Dances were usually arranged for a time when the moon was full. There was no street lighting, no battery torches. If the night was dark, the men brought stable lanterns. I had a small candle lantern, which would fit into my slipper bag. The ubiquitous leather hand-bag had not yet come into fashion.

The memory of those moonlight nights will ever remain with me. Against a clear sky, the dark trees were etched in their stark beauty. Twinkling diamonds of frost sparkled on the surface of the pond, rivalling the myriads of stars which glittered above. The air was vibrant, and the scene had a magical quality. Above the vaulted heavens, one could sense the boundless space, beyond human ken, where worlds, as yet unknown, pursued their destined revolutions, the music of the spheres unheard. Awed by the wonder of creation, how insignificant one felt, a tiny atom in the illimitable universe, yet able to sense its glory, to revel in its beauty.

While Ernest was still on vacation from College he reached his twenty first birthday. His parents gave a party, to which I was invited. I had spent one or two evenings previously at the Woods home when Ernest had entertained us with music, either on the organ in the adjacent Church, or on the piano. Often he played his own compositions. Sometimes he played the 'cello, when I would accompany him, somewhat diffidently, I must admit, on the piano. These were pleasant evenings and I always enjoyed them. Ernest's father was a kindly man, quiet and somewhat reserved. Not so his mother. Mrs Wood was a fussy, fidgety type, and a great chatterer. Her eyes were constantly upon me, anxious and watchful. She was like a mother hen fussing over her one chick, aware of danger and wondering how to avert it. Was Ernest getting too involved with this girl?

He spent a lot of time with her, and she was really a stranger. Little was known of her, or of her background. All this I could read as plainly as if printed, in her worried maternal eyes.

I wished that I could relieve her anxiety. As far as I was concerned our friendship was purely platonic. Ernest's musical ability I greatly admired, and we were enjoying a very pleasant companionship. He was a little younger than I, and to me seemed very immature, undoubtedly still tied very securely to his mother's apron strings. Mrs Wood really had no cause to worry as far as I was concerned.

At Ernest's birthday party I had been introduced to his great friend George. George was several years older than Ernest and lived with his widowed mother. He was regarded by the villagers as a confirmed bachelor. George had a great sense of fun and was very good company but I saw very little of him until Ernest's vacation came to an end.

In the first letter I received from Ernest, after his return to College, he wrote that he had asked George to look after me while he was away. Time sped by. Many social occasions other than dances were arranged in Tadley during the Autumn and Winter. They were held in the village school, and everyone, who was able, was called upon to help with the arrangements. Some decorated the room, others made cakes and other delicacies, or cut sandwiches. My contribution was the painting of gay posters, to advertise the event. Sometimes these social evenings were open to anyone, on payment of a shilling at the door. Some were by invitation only, the tickets then being three shillings and sixpence. All the functions were well attended, the proceeds being given to the Church or to some charity.

I usually went with Mr and Mrs Barrett, and often Mrs Barrett would give me a posy of sweet smelling early violets from her sheltered garden, to wear. She watched with a motherly eye as the friendship developed between Ernest and me. It evidently met with her approval, for several times she had invited us both to spend the evening at the schoolhouse.

Now, when George partnered me at dances and became my escort on other occasions, I could tell by Mrs Barrett's manner, that she was not very pleased. As nothing was said, I was not able to tell her that George was merely doing what Ernest had requested; but I had a feeling that she was disappointed in her protégé.

On Saturday afternoons when the weather was fine, George and I would cycle the seven miles into the nearest town to make a few purchases, and have a cup of tea before returning. I was very glad of his presence one day on our return journey. It was almost dark, and from the woods that we were passing, came a most alarming shriek. Had I been alone, I should have imagined murder being done, and cycled madly home with terror in my heart.

George laughed at my fears. 'It was only an owl' he said. I could hardly believe that such a fearsome sound could issue from the small throat of a bird.

Naturally the tongues in the village began to wag when George and I were seen together so frequently. He had never before paid serious attention to a girl. Was the bachelor to become a Benedick at last? Their speculations were in vain. George was completely loyal to Ernest. He told me, what I already knew, that Ernest had put me in his care, telling him that I was the girl he hoped to marry, but that he could not do anything about it for the present, as he had nothing to offer. He would have to wait until he had left College and had a settled position but he was afraid that in the meantime I might find somebody else. George's guardianship, he hoped, would help to avoid this. Having made our relationship quite clear, George and I were very happy in each other's company, for there was a greater affinity between us than between Ernest and myself. Although George must have been aware of the gossip we evoked, he ignored it and our pleasant companionship continued. In this way time passed quickly and happily until once again it was Christmas. I went home for the holiday to find that Stanley and Annie had already arrived. Stanley from College in London, Annie from the Midlands where she had been a Head Mistress for some years. When I had been about to leave College she had suggested that I should apply to fill a vacancy in her school. This I had done but my application was unsuccessful. To my surprise I now found at home a letter awaiting me from the Warwickshire Education Committee, the authority under which Annic had her headship. In it I was offered a post in a new school which was to be opened at Easter in the North of the County. An application form was enclosed.

Mother was delighted at the idea. Not only would my salary be increased to £80 per annum, but I should be near Annie, who could keep an eye on me—the very last thing I wanted—in fact, the more I thought over the project, the less I liked it. I was so happy at Tadley, with the place, and the people, that I could not imagine saying 'Goodbye' to it all. The very thought depressed me profoundly. Mother and Annie, of course, could not understand my attitude.

They pressed me to accept at once, but I put off making my decision, hoping against hope, that something would turn up, to prevent my going. Why could I not say outright, that I would not go? How ridiculous it seems in this age of independent free expression to think that even at the age of twenty one, it was not possible for me to please myself.

From babyhood, it had been impressed upon the family that mother and father knew best. They supplied our needs, physical and cultural, and we must follow the code of conduct laid down by them. We owed them a duty, which lay in deferring to their wishes, and never causing them worry. Duty, a word which seems to have vanished from the modern vocabulary, was then used as a moral cudgel. We were continually reminded of the duty we owed to God, to our parents, our school and our country. To fail in any of these was to stray from the 'straight and narrow path.' It was because of this deeply ingrained sense of duty, that I knew, in spite of my own wishes, that I must do what Mother suggested.

So the application form was duly filled in and sent. At the end of the holiday I set out for Tadley with a heavy heart, knowing with regret that it would be for the last time. As only one month's notice was needed, I decided to delay this as long as possible. In the meantime I determined to enjoy to the full the time that was left to me. But with the ever present thought of my impending departure much of the anticipated pleasure lost its savour. At last I had to tender my resignation. As I had feared, it was received with surprise and dismay by Mr and Mrs Barrett. What had happened they wanted to know. Was I not happy? I had seemed so settled and content. I assured them that I had been most happy, having received nothing but kindness. They were told of the letter, how it was not my wish but in deference to my parents that I was taking this step.

The Vicar visited me in an effort to persuade me to cancel my application. He had looked up particulars of the village to which I was going. A mining village he told me, with a nearby river which flooded acres of the surrounding land, different indeed he said from your beloved Sussex hills or this delightful spot which you are leaving. The picture was not an alluring one but I had said I would go. I had been taught to honour my word 'even though it were to my own hindrance.'

When Ernest came home for the Easter vacation he sought me at the first opportunity. I thought I had prepared him in my frequent letters for my leaving, but he was most upset to learn that I had really resigned. Again I was asked why? and again I had to explain that it was not my wish but that of my parents. Evidently unaware that he was himself so much under the jurisdiction of his mother, he told me that I was weak and foolish to give way against my own inclination.

Stammering with emotion he told me how much I meant to him, how he had thought of me constantly since we first met. Now, if I left Tadley his vacations which had afforded him so much happiness would become a dreary waste, his hopes would be dashed. Of these hopes for the future he had not meant to tell me so soon but my going was a bomb that had forced the issue. Dare he hope that one day, when circumstances made it possible, I would consent to marry him. Although I knew that Ernest had this in mind I had not imagined that I should be called upon to make so sudden a decision. As I murmured 'I don't know' Ernest took me in his arms and kissed me but, with cheeks suffused with blushes, I was too shy to reciprocate.

With his unanswered question heavy on my mind, it was long before sleep came to me that night. My thoughts were confused. Somewhere there lurked a tiny bubble of gratification at the proposal, but the pervading feeling was not one of jubilation. A small cloud dimmed the sunlit world in which I now existed. After my sheltered restricted youth I was thoroughly enjoying my new found independence. Nor yet did I wish to relinquish any part of it. If I became engaged to Ernest I should once more be subjected to the whims and desires of another entity. This would no doubt have been an added pleasure if I had been in love with Ernest but I realised that my feeling for him was not of this nature. I liked him, enjoyed his attentions, admired his musical ability but the vital spark was missing.

Each day Ernest met me as I came from school, also the small amount of leisure time that remained before my departure was spent together. When he again asked for an answer to his question I temporized, saying I was still thinking about it. For the moment that seemed to satisfy him. It was with a sad heart that I went round the village saying 'Goodbye' to the many kind people I had met. The last week came all too soon. I was leaving on Saturday but, on Friday evening I went as usual to choir practice. When, among the hymns to be sung on Sunday I found that one was for 'absent friends' the tears came to my eyes.

# 9. *Changing scene*

WOODEND, THOUGH IT was indeed a mining village, did not belie its name for it lay among pleasantly wooded country, a veritable 'cinder in a bouquet.'

'Digs' had been found for me with Mrs Brandrick, who kept the village shop. As the Vicar had surmised, the environment was a strange one. The sound of the heavily shod feet of the miners, on their way in the very early morning, was a complete contrast to the lowing of cattle, and the bleating of sheep.

Strange too, I found the sight of the men coming home with their blackened faces. This was long before the era of pit-head baths. It was the wives' duty to keep the men clean. The washing copper was filled, the fires beneath them stoked up, water hot, ready for the returning men. Through the uncurtained windows of the wash-houses, it was a common sight to see the men stripped to the waist, standing by the sink, while the wives vigorously applied a soapy flannel to their grimy backs.

Most of the wives were very house proud. The curtains and windows were kept immaculate, floors and furniture well polished. Brass ornaments, of which they were very fond, gleamed and twinkled in the fire light. The free allowance of coal which they were granted, always ensured a good fire in the bright cosy homes. There were, of course, some shiftless wives, whose homes and gardens were a sorry mess, but these were in the minority.

In the summer, between shifts, the men would sit by the roadside, their legs dangling over a dry ditch, smoking, spitting, laughing and chaffing together. Some of them gave a hand to the local farmers, particularly at harvest time.

My 'digs' were comfortable, and the school was most attractive. There were two other assistants besides the Headmistress and myself. We each had our own classroom, which was quite unusual as far as I was concerned, as was the clean new equipment. From the window on one side, I watched a damson tree break into blossom against a grey spring sky. From the windows on the other side could be seen the wood, from which the village took its name, so the prospect was not so drab as the Vicar had supposed.

I appreciated working in a modern school for besides a separate classroom, both Headmistress and Staff had a room to which they could retire, and also a cloakroom fitted with 'mod. cons,' so different from my former lack of amenities. Unfortunately, our comfort was marred by the disposition of the Headmistress, Miss Skimpton. She was a thin, acidulated spinster, about fifty, undoubtedly frustrated, neurotic, and at a trying period of her life. She tried in every possible way to repress our high spirits, finding fault without cause, but never praising. She had the pernicious habit of criticising one member of the Staff to the others, but we were all young and friendly together. This helped us to endure her carping ways.

In the long evenings, I explored the surrounding country on my bicycle, and found it more pleasant than I had anticipated. The land was undulating, with many woods and little copses. There were fewer wild flowers in the verges; I also missed the 'Old man's Beard' which romped and burgeoned over the hedges in my chalky home County.

I found much to write about to Winifred, Ernest, and to my Mother, in my weekly letters home. The people were a source of great interest to me. Their community of interests provided a constant topic of conversation. They quarrelled, and bickered, but when trouble or sickness came, neighbourly help was always forthcoming. Mrs Brandrick, my landlady, kept me well informed about village gossip, which she had, first hand, from her customers.

At first, I listened with interest to her colourful account of the life of the villagers. Such uninhibited exposure of intimate details was new to me; it often raised a blush to my cheeks. The reserve which I had always known, simply didn't exist, I was made aware of many new facets of human behaviour. Some I found most shocking, but many were extremely amusing. As Mrs Brandrick babbled on,

I made no comment. She expected none. I sometimes wondered how long she could have continued without interruption. Fortunately, it was seldom long before the shop bell tinkled, and she was recalled to her duties.

When the summer holiday came, I felt that my first term at Woodend had certainly increased my knowledge of life as it is lived.

The nearest railway station was about five miles away, so when starting for home I ordered the only transport available in the village. This was a high trap driven by a wild looking woman named Mrs Cutler. She was tall and gaunt. Her large hat was securely skewered to her big bun by four long murderous looking hat pins, the sharp ends of which protruded for several inches. No charioteer could have been prouder, or behaved with more abandon than Mrs Cutler when she held the reins. With her hat flapping backwards against the restraining pins, she brandished her whip over Blossom, the horse, meanwhile shouting weird and unintelligible sounds of encouragement. Blossom, no longer young, had one pace, regardless of the threats and entreaties of the would be Jehu. In spite of everything, Mrs Cutler had never been known to miss a train.

When returning to Woodend, I always had to change at Rugby, and wait a weary hour. I had made this journey several times. Then on one occasion, when I was pacing up and down, I saw a familiar figure. Yes, it was Dash, who had sat behind me in College. She too, was waiting for a train to Nuneaton. Although Dash and I had not known each other particularly well in College, we were both delighted to see a familiar face; the time of waiting passed in a flash. Before we parted, we had agreed to visit each other. I was first to spend a week-end with her. This I did a few weeks later, and had a very pleasant time. In the morning, we went round the shops, in the evening to the Cinema, something not possible in Woodend.

Dash paid a return visit soon afterwards, when we had a really hectic time. About a mile from our village was a much bigger and livelier one named Hurley. On the Friday night we went to a dance held in the schoolroom there. I had already met the schoolmaster, to whom I introduced Dash. During the course of the evening he asked if we would like to drive on Saturday morning into Tamworth, as he and his wife would be going. Their way lay through Woodend, so they would pick us up there. We readily agreed, thoroughly enjoying the ride, and the visit to the pleasant little Market Town. Our vehicle was a 'tub' with comfortable cushioned seats, very different from the slippery precarious perch in Mrs Cutler's trap.

In the afternoon, I borrowed a bicycle for Dash, and we cycled to Kingsbury, a still bigger village, which was about three miles away, for tennis. The tennis court was in the schoolhouse garden; I had been invited to play there anytime I wished. The schoolmaster, Mr Wallace, his wife, also their two sons, were keen players. Dash was made welcome, and we played until tea time. We were invited into the schoolhouse for tea, after which we left regretfully, as I had promised that we would attend a Whist Drive in our own village that evening.

On Sunday morning Mrs Brandrick gave us our breakfast in bed. We got up in time for Church, then after lunch went for a walk through the wood and round the lanes. After an early tea, Mrs Cutler and Blossom arrived to take Dash to the station. Dash had suggested that it would be nice if we could both teach in the same place, and share 'digs.' She was thinking of my going to Nuneaton, where she said vacancies did sometimes occur. However, after her week-end with me she wrote 'I think your life in Woodend is pleasanter, and much fuller than mine, how about my joining you there?' I was quite agreeable. Life in this small community suited me much better than life in town. Here, I felt close to the human drama. I had been accepted by the village; the women spoke to me freely about their personal relationships, their worries, perplexities and ambitions. Sometimes, listening to the difficulties with which these women had to cope, some of whom were little older than myself, I felt that I was merely skimming the surface of life. What hidden depths I wondered lay beneath for me.

During all this time, I was receiving lengthy letters from Ernest twice a week. His account of College life, I found most interesting, and often amusing. The escapades, in which the male students engaged, were certainly more daring, and hazardous, than those perpetrated by us when in College. What disturbed me, however, was the fact that his letters were becoming more ardent. My feelings towards him had not changed; I was convinced that I ought to make this clear to him, before he left College. How to do it without hurting him was the question. I had hoped that the tone of my letters would have been sufficient, but it evidently was not so. Supposing I refused Ernest, and no one else ever asked me? Women far outnumbered men: I thought of all the unmarried teachers I knew. Would Ernest's devotion, supposing it endured, together with our mutual love of music, be a good enough foundation for a happy marriage, for we had little else in common, apart from our interest in teaching. Many fundamental things had seldom been discussed between us, because of our widely differing views. Surely in a perfect marriage, mind and body both should be attuned. Perhaps such an ideal was unattainable, a mere figment of the imagination. If only I were in love with Ernest, such considerations would no doubt have been cast to the winds. The pity was, that all I felt for him was affection. Could this affection possibly develop into love.?

I wrote to Winifred, and put the problem before her, begging her to resolve it for me. Very wisely she replied that it was something I must settle for myself. After much more thought, I finally made up my mind and wrote to Ernest giving him my decision. When he was free from home and College, I wrote, I was sure he would meet many girls who would appeal to him as much as I had done, I hoped he would find one who would reciprocate his devotion, as he deserved.

He replied by return, a letter full of distress and pleading, which brought tears to my eyes. I thought again how sensible I had been in not meeting him, or I should have weakened. Each day brought an imploring letter, begging that my decision should not be final, that I would at least continue our correspondence. To this I agreed, thinking that my letters could perhaps prove an inclined plane, down which I could gradually bring him out of the clouds, and back to earth. I was glad that I had agreed, for we were still writing, but with less frequency until the outbreak of the first world war, when I received the sad news that Ernest had been one of its earliest victims.

# 10. *Dash*

At last the vacancy that Dash had been waiting for occurred at Hurley school. Mr Jackson, the headmaster, was delighted when she put in an application, which was accepted. Mrs Brandrick, my landlady, did not feel that she could cope with another lodger, as she was pregnant. She felt that with the shop, she really had enough to do. As our idea was to live together, Dash and I sought other 'digs,' and found them in Hurley, with a Mrs Tasker, a big woman, with a large, round fleshy face. She was always enveloped in a voluminous white apron, and was very deaf. An unmarried daughter Ada, waited on us, prim and abrupt, and seemingly resentful. She hardly spoke, quite unlike Mrs Tasker, who babbled on and on unceasingly. It was useless trying to answer her, for to anything we said, she gave such surprisingly inept replies, that we could scarcely restrain our mirth. We were always in a state of repressed giggles whenever she was present.

Her recently acquired artificial teeth were constantly brought to our attention. Whenever she paused for breath, she would champ and gnash these dentures together, as if with enjoyment. Often she held in one hand a box of matches, the rough side of this she would rub over her other horny palm. The gnashing of the teeth, with the rasping of the match box, provided a percussion accompaniment to her flat and monotonous monologue, which caused us great amusement.

Opposite our 'digs' was a tiny Chapel but the Church was half a mile away in the centre of the village. The Church was in change of a Curate, who lived in the adjoining Parsonage, with his wife and baby. He was young, good looking and very musical. Soon he invited Dash and me to join his small choir. This we agreed to do, making up the number to six. The four others were all young men. The practices were held in the Parsonage. One evening Mr Evans, the Curate, said he had an idea that we might do something to raise funds for the Church, which was a small wooden building with a corrugated roof, sadly in need of repair, and decoration. His idea was, that we should form a concert party. We were all enthusiastic, and various names were suggested for the group. We finally decided on the Fol-de-Rols. Our costumes were to be pink, with black pompoms, and conical hats. Dash and I were to have knee length skirts.

The practices were great fun. Not only was the Curate a splendid musician, he could improvise, compose words and music. play by ear, but best of all, he had a wonderful sense of humour. Our repertoire consisted of patriotic songs, ballads, serious and gay. Some were so saucy that I wondered at their inclusion.

To vary the programme, we thought of a One Act Play. The versatile Mr Evans soon produced a suitable one, and rehearsals began. With the introduction of an odd song, and recitations by local talent, our Programme was complete.

Dash and I were rather perturbed at the shortness of our skirts. Our usual ones, at this time, were quite long, not even our ankles showed, but, in the short pink ones, even our knees would be exposed. We had made petticoats with multiple frills to wear under the skirts. Long white stockings, and white shoes with a pompom on the toe completed our costume.

The concert was to be given on two consecutive nights, Friday and Saturday. A stage was erected at the far end of the schoolroom and, as there were no curtains, screens would be placed at the sides, to be used when necessary. When the night arrived, the villagers flocked in. A concert was a rare event, and they were looking forward to hearing songs in ragtime, which was still a novelty.

One of the items, between the Fol-de-Rols, and the sketch, was sung by an elderly spinster. She had a forbidding appearance, but a very pleasing voice. Her choice of song was 'One night of love.' Looking at her, Dash said to me, 'My word, she's a dark horse.' The contrast between her severe mien, and the rapture and abandon of which she sang, was so ludicrous, that we both collapsed with laughter. The concert was voted a great success, so on the Saturday

evening the room was filled to capacity. Someone remarked faceti-
ously that the males in the audience had come to see the girls' legs and
frillies, but we preferred to think that it was the novelty of the entertainment, that had attracted their support.

Dash and I were very fond of dancing and this soon became known.
One evening we were invited to supper at one of the local farm-
houses. It was not very far away, but was at the end of a lane, which
was always very muddy. The road too was muddy, so we decided to
walk, rather than risk the hazard of deep muddy ruts, on our bicycles.
We took our candle lanterns, and set out, our feet well shod in our
high leather boots.

We were surprised to find quite a party awaiting us. Besides our
host and hostess, there were also two other farmers and their wives.
To us, the supper was a banquet. There was a boiled fowl, covered
with a decorated white sauce, a luscious home cured ham, raised
pork pie, sausage rolls with, to accompany them, jacketed potatoes
and pickles as well as chutneys in variety. For sweets there were
bottled damsons, with thick cream, some jam and lemon cheese
tarts, with local cheese to follow. We heaved a sigh, as we finished,
the delicious meal, so different from the food provided by Mrs Tasker
who was a poor and unimaginative cook.

After the meal, we were told the reason for the party. They
wanted to enlist our help. The three neighbours had met previously,
to discuss ways of providing more entertainment in the village.
Dances were very popular, but infrequent; they wondered if it
would be possible, to hold them weekly. There were many new
dances they would like to learn, but to do so necessitated a teacher.
To get one from Town would be expensive, as it would probably
be necessary for the instructor to be accommodated for the night.
Now they wondered if Dash and I would be willing to give weekly
lessons. The farmers would form a Committee and help in every
possible way. A few meetings would be necessary, before starting
the dances, to decide about dates, music, price and other incidentals.
The meetings, to which we were invited, would be held in each of
their homes in turn.

Dash and I readily agreed to help. The thought of a weekly dance
delighted us; we felt that the teaching would be no problem, with
pupils willing and eager to learn. We were then driven home in a
snug 'tub' and transport was provided for the subsequent meetings.
At each of these we enjoyed such a delectable repast, that we were

almost sorry when the meetings ended, and the dances were ready
to begin.

A local pianist had been found, who was willing to oblige, for
quite a small fee: Tom Dowser the village blacksmith, had offered
his services free, just for the pleasure of playing his violin. Any one
less like a 'mighty' blacksmith 'with broad and sinewy hands' it
would be difficult to imagine. Tom was a short nonentity of a man,
with sparse wispy hair on top of which he usually wore a slightly
small and well worn bowler hat. Even when playing, he occasionally forgot to remove it. He never appeared without his wife. As he
was short, he stood upon a bench to play. His tone was squeaky, but
his timing excellent. Below him, on the bench, sat his wife, stiff and
unyielding. Corsets encased her like armour, her black frock fitted
like a skin. Her grey hair was strained tightly back into a bun, the
neatness of which was assured by the copious use of thick black hair-
pins. She never smiled, but sat there, stern and uncompromising,
throughout every session.

It was said that she came to keep here eye on Tom: she wasn't
going to have him making eyes at the girls. Poor Tom! Did she regard
him as an Adonis, and irresistible, or was there some incident in a
murky past that warranted such vigilance? We never knew.

The classes were held each Friday night; we taught the Valeta,
La Rinka, a simple Tango, with one or two others that were fairly
new, and we polished up the Waltz, and the Lancers.

Twice during the season we had a 'Grand Ball.' Everything just
a little better than usual was termed 'Grand.' Our 'Grand Ball' was
very little different from the Friday hops. The floor of the schoolroom remained rough and splintery, in spite of the copious sprinkling
of powder. The orchestra still consisted of the pianist and Tom, with
his fiddle. There were a few differences however, for one thing,
breeches and leggings were 'out,' the men came in dark suits, a few
even rose to dinner jackets. Instead of tweed skirts and blouses, the
ladies wore dresses. Most of these were simple dresses that had done
duty in the summer, but a few, worn by the more prosperous members of the community, were of silk or satin. Some of the ladies even
sported a fan.

There were many amusing incidents at the dances. One, which
delighted us, was when Bill Yardley's false shirt front, his dicky,
slipped from its moorings, and slowly emerged, inch by inch below
his waistcoat. It descended slowly, until at last Bill became aware

of its odd position, and beat a hasty retreat to the cloakroom.

Sometimes we were invited to dances at Kingsbury, where we played tennis in the summer. It was a much bigger village than Hurley, and the dances were more sophisticated, although they too, were held in a schoolroom. There was a better floor, and a proper dance orchestra was engaged. Having been to several dances there, in our only evening dresses, Dash and I felt we should like to go in something different—but what? and how? that was the question. Funds were low—they always were—and pay day wasn't till after one such event. Dash had an idea 'Suppose' she said, 'I write to Ellie.' Ellie was a friend who had been on the same staff, at Nuneaton. 'Ellie,' she went on 'has heaps of clothes and I am sure she would help if she could.'

The letter was sent. In a few days a parcel arrived. We opened it excitedly, not knowing what to expect. Inside were two evening dresses, both of satin, one blue and one white. They seemed much the same size, which was a pity, as I was several inches taller than Dash. As the white one seemed slightly smaller, Dash decided on that. She tried it on. It reached to the ground, and being full, looked, on her, like an outsize nightgown. Undismayed, she said that a good hem would take care of the length; with a belt, the extra fullness could be controlled.

Then I put on the blue one. It barely reached my ankles, far from needing to be pulled in, it clasped me tight. We looked at each other and burst into fits of laughter. 'Really, Dash' I said 'I don't think we can possibly wear these.' 'Don't be silly, wait till I've turned up this hem, and you've put on some thinner underclothes, they'll look very different then' she said confidently.

I was still unconvinced. They were pretty dresses, although not what we should have chosen; by no stretch of the imagination could they have been called a good fit, but we decided to wear them.

As far as we knew, no one else from Hurley was going to the dance so we should have no company on the way. The evening was fine but cloudy, so we decided to walk. By the road it was about two miles, but there was a short cut across the fields.

Before starting, we put a broad elastic band round our waists. Into this we tucked the bottom of the dresses, to keep them well out of the mud. They must not even come into contact with our boots, which it was necessary to wear, when crossing the fields. Our dance shoes were ready in our slipper bags, to change into on arrival.

There was a slight drizzle before we finished our journey, the short ends of hair, beneath our hats, hung in damp ringlets. In the cloakroom we changed our shoes, and dried our faces. Thanks to the drizzle, they were now devoid of powder and shone with a rubicund glow. Powder was only used in one's bedroom, and had not yet made its appearance in public places. We could do little but tidy our damp hair, so pressing the creases from our frocks as best we could, we made our way to the dance floor.

We were received by the promoter, a very soigné lady. Round her immaculate head she wore a ribbon, from which three aigrettes sprouted erect. In one of her gloved hands she held a fan. Her smart evening gown sparkled with irridescent sequins. Looking round the room, I saw many fashionable dresses, and wished fervently that I had been wearing my own, which, even if well worn, did at least fit.

Several times during the evening, I caught sight of Dash in her ample bride like garment, and thinking how odd, I too, must look, I chuckled to myself. If we did look figures of fun, we could enjoy the joke. Perhaps we were over critical, for we had a very jolly evening, with a partner for every dance, and several offers of company on the way home. These we refused. The night was now fine, the moon was shining, and we were not nervous.

One man, however, refused to take 'No' for an answer and insisted on accompanying us. He was a stranger to us, but we had been introduced to him, and he had danced with each of us. We knew that he would be well known to the organisers of the dance, for those invited were always carefully selected: much heart burning was caused among those to whom an invitation was not extended. We did not welcome his company, and wondered why he had persisted. Perhaps he was merely being gentlemanly, or maybe he enjoyed a moonlight walk through muddy fields. We hoped so, for that was the only satisfaction he got.

We entered the house quietly. We did not want to waken Ada, her looks were sour enough, without any further provocation. Mrs Tasker, we knew, would not be disturbed by any noise we could make. While I lit the candle placed ready for us, Dash went into the kitchen for a drink of water. The moon gave enough light to discern the outline of things. Picking up a cup from the draining board she emptied the contents into the sink. Oh! Gosh! she said, "There was something in it.' I took the candle, to see what was the matter.

To our dismay, we saw, lying in the sink, the well known dentures of Mrs Tasker. Fortunately, they were unbroken, so, with a feeling of distaste, we restored them to the cup. Never, indeed, had we anticipated a personal contact with Mrs Tasker's gnashers. Suddenly it struck us as funny, and we held on to each other, as we shook with suppressed laughter.

Before Dash came, while I was still at Woodend, I had often attended an ancient Church in a nearby hamlet. It was surrounded by delightful country; the Church itself being approached by an avenue of limes. Unfortunately, these had been pollarded, so the delicious fragrance of their blossoms no longer scented the summer air.

There were only a few cottages and a farmhouse near the Church, the main part of the village being about a mile away. Here, there was quite a cluster of houses, some of them being fairly new. There was also a public house, a blacksmith's forge, and a general shop. Cricket was played on the village green, and there was also a tennis court, on which I had occasionally played.

Dash was very keen on tennis, so we decided to join the Club which existed here. Among the members were two brothers, who often partnered us. Don was tall and fair; Howard, the younger, was short and dark; we greatly enjoyed our mixed doubles.

We also made friends with a young married woman, Betty Braithwaite, petite and pretty. She was a Yorkshirewoman, and most hospitable. We were frequently invited to tea—a real meal! When she heard that we had no bathroom in the 'digs' she insisted that we should use hers. How gladly we accepted the kind offer, but we were much exercised as to how we could repay so much kindness.

We knew that she enjoyed our company, for she was a merry little soul, and we had a lot of fun together. She did not make friends readily, and we had sensed that the husband and wife relationship was not as happy as it might have been. On the few occasions on which we met Mr Braithwaite, he seemed abrupt and morose, with no apparent sense of humour. We knew that few of his evenings were spent at home, but many at the local inn.

Before being asked to join the choir at Hurley, we preferred to walk through the fields to the ancient Church which Don and Howard also attended. Often, after the evening service, they would walk back with us to Hurley. Their home was a creeper covered farm house near the Church. At the back of the house, in the meadow by the orchard, they had made a tennis court, where we were invited to play. This was even better than the Club, for we could play continuously. On many of the long summer evenings, we played set after set, until the light failed. Then we sat under the trees, to refresh ourselves with glasses of milk or lemonade: we rarely went into the house, unless the midges were too troublesome. Living with the family was a distant cousin, Miss Tait. Her age, we thought, was somewhere between fifty and sixty. For many years she had looked after an aged and ailing mother. When she died, Miss Tait had come to live with the Osbornes, her only relatives. She was reputed to be wealthy, but mean. We thought her very odd. In each ear, she had a wad of cotton wool, a permanent appendage. She took her meals with the family, but her remarks were few, and as soon as the meal ended, she returned to her own rooms. Her only companion was a small black pomeranian dog. Tiny was old and smelly, and Miss Tait herself was not above suspicion in this respect. Her heavy silk dress, the only one we ever saw her wear, was dark grey, it seemed such a part of her, that we wondered if she ever took it off. We were appalled at her solitary life, immured in her room; but Miss Tait was not a person with whom one could sympathize, she was far too forbidding.

We were really sorry for Tiny, the poor obese little creature was definitely short of exercise. One day, when we had been invited to a meal, we managed to accost Miss Tait, before she disappeared, and asked if we might take Tiny for a walk. To our surprise, her eyes lit up and she agreed. After that, we often took him for a run, well not exactly a run, but a sedate waddle round the fields. Following one of these excursions, we were invited into Miss Tait's room, to the great surprise of the family, for such a thing was unprecedented.

What a hotchpotch the room was. It was absolutely filled to capacity. There was scarcely room to move between the furniture. trunks, boxes, and other impedimenta. On the mantel, and the tops of the chests were countless ornaments, photos, and other bric-a-brac. Scarcely any of the wallpaper could be seen, for the multiplicity of pictures, and framed family groups, which hung there. Overriding the fug and musty smell of the room, was an all pervading odour of moth balls.

Motioning us to a seat, Miss Tait took from her pocket a large housekeeping purse. From this, she extracted a bunch of keys. She sorted out the one necessary, and unlocked the top drawer in one of the chests. From this, she produced a small mahogany box, inlaid with mother of pearl. Taking from it a miniature in a pierced gold frame, she handed it to us. We saw, depicted in delicate colours, an elderly woman with aquiline features 'My Mother' she said. From the box she also took a cameo brooch, a garnet necklace, and other jewellery, which she said, her mother had worn.

Then, kneeling, she lifted the lid of a carved oak chest and held up, for our inspection, the very gown pictured in the miniature. It had a paisley design, and was tucked and befrilled. The bodice narrowed into the waist; the workmanship was exquisite. We examined it with admiration. Then, she produced one bigger and more voluminous. 'This' she said 'was worn by my grandmother.' It was a beautiful gown. The soft fine woolly material was of a creamy colour, scattered with charming posies in their natural colours. We held both of them up, and looked at them almost with veneration. We watched Miss Tait replace them, lock and counter lock her treasures, as we thanked here sincerely for allowing us to see her valued possessions.

Time passed quickly, the long summer holiday came and went, and we were back again ready for our autumn programme. This included the renewal of the weekly dances. Except for individual attention to the few new members, Dash and I had little teaching to do, for the regular attenders had now become expert.

To provide interest, and enliven the usual 'Grand' dances, we decided to hold a Fancy Dress Ball. To pay for the added expense of decorating the room, and hiring an orchestra, invitations were sent to the neighbouring villages. Among those invited were the Breedens They had lived in Hurley for a long time, but had left the village shortly before our arrival, and now lived at Dunton. We were constantly being told 'What a pity you didn't come before the Breedens left.' They had made a great impression upon the village. Tales were still told of the wonderful wedding of one of the aunts, when the bride was driven to the mother Church at Kingsbury, four miles away, in a carriage and pair, with a postillion and out riders. Besides the family, there were many relatives living near, aunts, uncles, cousins to the Nth degree. When they attended any village function, the success, numerically, at least, was always assured.

The idea of the Fancy Dress captured the imagination of our clientele who, at once, began to think of the costumes they would acquire. Almost simultaneously, the thought of Miss Tait's lovely dresses, occurred to Dash and myself. Supposing we could borrow them, would it be sacrilege to wear them for such an occasion. Anyway, it was extremely unlikely that she would allow us to borrow her prized possessions. Greatly daring, we decided to put it to the test. To our surprise, and great delight, she agreed to lend them. We promised to treat them with the utmost care, and bore them away, hoping fervently that we should be able to get into them.

When we tried them on, and found that we could indeed wear them, we felt that magic was at work, and we called down blessings on Miss Tait and her ancestors.

The scene at the dance was a gay one. Never before had such an event been held at Hurley, and everyone seemed determined to make it a success. There were costumes in great variety. Some were home made, contrived out of oddments, others had been hired from the Town, at considerable expense. Henry VIII arrived most resplendent with jewelled trappings. There was Mary, Queen of Scots, demure in black velvet, and a scarlet Mephistopheles, complete with horns, making great play with his sinuous tail. Some characters were difficult to name among the many well known pierrots, gipsies, pirates, and Dutch girls.

The fun waxed fast and furious. Most of the dances required quite a lot of energy, and the well filled room became very hot. At one point, I was amused by the sight of King Charles, minus his wig, mopping his streaming brow. The large florid countenance of the farmer, arising from the lacey furbelows, looked strangely odd, as did the sight of the long black curly wig, dangling ludicrously from his knee.

Four of the Breeden family came, bringing with them a group of young people from their village, all in fancy dress. John, the eldest of the Breeden boys asked me for a dance, and, at its conclusion, asked if he could have the next, but, as we sat and chatted I told him this was impossible. Several of the members of the regular Friday 'hops' would be hurt if they didn't have at least one dance with their instructress. Don and Howard too, were present and would expect dances. John said he was sorry they had left Hurley so soon, for it had certainly wakened up since Dash and I had come. With dances, concerts and a Pierrot Troupe it had become so lively that it made their new village seem dull. They were, however, having a Whist Drive soon, and he would see that Dash and I were invited.

The invitation, to the Whist Drive and Dance, duly arrived, not by post, as we had anticipated, but in person, the following Saturday. We had cycled into Tamworth in the morning to do some shopping, and had returned to a late lunch. Just as we were finishing, we heard the Clop! Clop! of a horse, which suddenly stopped. From the window, we saw John tethering his horse to the front railings.

Fortunately Ada was out, and we were able to let John in, without Mrs Tasker's knowledge. She had never commented on the occasional visits of Don and Howard, but we felt that if the number of male visitors increased, Ada might have some unpleasant remarks to make.

We accepted the invitation, and John said that several other people from Hurley, had also received invitations. Next morning we met the Ellises, who were on the dance Committee, with whom we had become friendly. They asked if we would like to drive to Dunton with them, an offer which we gladly accepted. It saved the necessity of cycling and, if the weather should be unkind, arriving in a somewhat dishevelled state.

We then set to work to finish off some dresses that we were in the process of making. Mine was of tussore silk, with a panel of Liberty embroidery down the left side. Dash had made hers of blue cashmere with the hem at the side front caught up to show a few inches of lace trimmed petticoat. We thought this rather daring, wondering once or twice, whether to replace it by the usual hem. In the end, it was left with the petticoat coyly peeping. Both dresses were finished in time to wear to the Whist Drive and Dance at Dunton.

Although we had often cycled through this village on the way to Birmingham, we had not before attended any function there. John met us at the door, and, as we entered the schoolroom, we could feel many curious eyes upon us. This was hardly surprising, as quite a proportion of those assembled were relatives of John. His father and mother, two aunts and an uncle, his sisters and brothers, were all there. Those we had not already met, were naturally interested to see the girls whom John had specially invited.

After the Whist, while the tables were cleared away, and the floor swept ready for the dancing, John introduced us to his parents. His father we liked at once. He was tall, with thick grey hair. His face was long, but his cheeks were rosy, his blue eyes looked at us with a twinkle. Mrs Breeden was aloof, rather supercilious we thought. As her eyes looked us up and down, we wondered if our dresses looked home made, and Dash said afterwards that she was sure the sight of her petticoat frill, was viewed with disdain. Frigid or friendly, we were not greatly concerned. Coming events, had not yet thrown any shadow.

# 11. The Swains

For some time we had been dissatisfied with out 'digs.' When as a result of Mrs Tasker's atrocious catering, I had a severe tummy upset, we decided to make a move. When we told Mrs Braithwaite, Betty, as we now called her, she at once said "Why not come here." We were delighted. The food we knew would be excellent, our baths would no longer be limited. The only snag was, that we should have a longer journey to school, each of us about four miles, but what was that on a bicycle. Regretfully we should have to give up the choir at Hurley but could still attend our favourite Church.

We gave the requisite notice to Mrs Tasker, and were soon comfortably installed with Betty. She seemed glad of our company. We saw little of her husband, for he was seldom at home. On the few occasions when we did see him, he was quite affable, and seemed to approve rather than resent our presence there.

On our way to school, Dash and I cycled about a mile together, before our paths divided. On the way we passed the farm where Don and Howard lived. As I taught in a junior school, I left earlier than Dash in the afternoon, and almost every day I saw Don, as I was returning home. He never seemed too busy for a chat. This surprised me, for I knew that he and his father were the main workers on the farm, with occasional help from Howard, when he was not studying.

Fortunately the winter proved a mild one. There was only one heavy fall of snow, which lay for about a week. This made the journey to school very tedious. It was impossible to cycle, for the snow in the country lanes, unpressed by traffic, clogged the mud guards, and stopped the wheels revolving. Walking was a discomfort, for the soft snow walked up the inside of our long skirts, and we arrived sodden. This necessitated a change of skirt, petticoat, and stockings. but we suffered no harm, for we were warmed by the exercise, and exhilerated by the clean crisp air.

To watch the coming of Spring was a joy. The "lambs tails" of the hazel dangled in the hedge, and spilled their yellow pollen on the breeze. The elder, and the honeysuckle broke into leaf, and the silver pussy willow gave promise of the golden glory to come. Blackthorn braved the cold, with its snowy blossoms, and the tall poplars were already tinged with colour. Soon the ground would be strewn with their handsome crimson catkins. In the fields the lambs skipped merrily, in spite of their plaintive cries. The birds with excessive energy flitted to and fro, often with streamers of nest building material trailing from their beaks, pausing now and then to fill the air with song.

We had played tennis through the winter, whenever it was possible, on the hard court at the Club. Don and Howard prepared their grass court as soon as the ground was dry, and we resumed our evenings of tennis there. They were excellent partners, not only for tennis but for dancing as well. They performed many little services for us, mending our punctures, often driving us to Concerts and Socials at a distance. Sometimes they would walk home with us on Sunday evenings after Church. Although we knew this gave rise to gossip, we were not concerned.

To our surprise, one Sunday evening, John Breeden and a friend came to our Church, which was one they had attended occasionally, when they lived at Hurley. John was waiting for us as we came out. He introduced us to his friend Harry who lived in Hurley, and was a school chum of his. They asked if they could walk home with us. We had no excuse to offer, so we started off. Don and Howard passed us with a curt "Good-night". John said he had driven with his father to visit the grandmother who still lived in Hurley village, They had come, he said, in their new Ford car, which he was learning to drive.

We were about to say 'Goodbye' as we reached the house, when Betty opened the door. "Oh!" she said "Are your friends coming in, I've just made some coffee." They needed no further inducement.

Soon Betty produced coffee and some of her delicious cakes. When they left, as they thanked her, she said she hoped they would come again. As soon as they had gone, she said to us, with a twinkle, "I wonder what Don and Howard will have to say." Naughty Betty! we knew that she had engineered what she thought might be an embarrassing situation, just for her own amusement.

She was disappointed, for the occasion caused no comment. Although we saw a lot of Don and Howard there was no reason why we should not have other friends. Our relationship was still on the plane of friendship, although I sometimes wondered about Dash and Howard. Howard did not appear to me at all prepossessing. He was dark, with a rather swarthy skin troubled by an eruption of adolescent pimples. Younger than Dash, he was still serving his apprenticeship to engineering. Don was tall with brown hair, and eyes which had a wistful and endearing look, like those of a spaniel.

A few days later John arrived again at the Braithwaites, this time on a bicycle. He had something to do in Hurley, he said, and he wondered if I would go with him for the walk there, as it was such a nice day. I put on some walking shoes, and we set out, ignoring the raised eyebrows of Betty.

When they left Hurley, John said they had let the farm, but had retained one field in which there was a small barn. Here John had some cattle of his own. The tenant farmer kept his eye on them, but John visited them frequently. We climbed a stile, and went down a narrow lane to the gate of the field. The calves came bounding towards us. They were Hereford bullocks, best of all for beef, John said. I liked their white faces, but was quite ignorant of any good or bad points they might possess. We did not go into the field, but as John seemed satisfied as to their well being, we retraced our steps. He would not come in, but was soon away on his bicycle. Betty, of course, was ready with her usual innuendos when I appeared.

During the summer, Dash and I spent an occasional week-end with my sister Annie, who lived about twenty miles away. We cycled after school on Friday, and back after tea on Sunday. Annie lived in the schoolhouse which was attached to her village school. One of her assistants, Miss Grey, lived with her. The schoolhouse was let with a modicum of furniture, to which Annie had added some nice pieces of her own. We admired Annie's taste, not only in furnishing, but in her dress. She was tall, with a good figure, and carriage, looking particularly well in tailor made suits. She introduced us to her tailor and we ordered a suit each. They were to cost £2.8.0d which we considered reasonable. The ones I had had made at home cost £3.3.0d in tweed, but £4.4.0d in smooth cloth.

The tailor said he would need two fittings, so that meant two more week-ends with Annie. These were always enjoyable, for we went shopping in the nearby town in the morning, often to the cinema in the afternoon. In the evening there was usually something on in the village. Annie did not come with us to these affairs; we went with Miss Grey, nor did Annie spend Sunday afternoon with us, but disappeared soon after lunch for some mysterious rendez-vous. We were never invited to accompany her, and our curiosity was aroused. Annie was very reserved. We knew we should glean nothing from her, so we bombarded poor Miss Grey with questions. We learnt that Annie was courting. Her suitor was a farmer's son. His father, a Scotsman, had come to England many years before and was farming in the locality.

We were greatly intrigued, and wished that we could catch sight of the elusive suitor. Somehow we had not associated Annie with the tender passion; we thought it clever of Cupid to plant a dart in what we had imagined to be a heart impervious to such things. In my next letter home, I imparted the news to mother, knowing how interested she would be, but asking her, under no circumstances to let Annie know that we had discovered her secret.

At the time appointed, we went to the tailors for out first fitting. We had our usual pleasant week-end but we gained no further information from Miss Grey about Annie's love affair, which she was apparently managing to keep discreetly hidden, even from the villagers.

When our final fitting at the tailors was due, the weather on Friday was dull and drizzly. We put on our drab mackintoshes and set out. On Saturday the weather was worse, and we cycled to the tailor's in the rain. We were very pleased with the look of the tweed costumes, which the tailor promised to post the following week.

Sunday was a real wet day, so we set off for home earlier than usual. As our macks did not seem to afford enough protection, Annie lent us each an old one, which we put on over our own. The rain didn't cease and what wind there was seemed to be blowing in our faces all the way. Water dripped into our boots, and ran off our chins. The going was heavy along the muddy roads. We were very hot inside the coats which were weighted with rain, but we were unable to discard anything. As we neared home, it became dark.

We dismounted to light our smelly little oil lamps. What a job this proved to be. The heads broke off the damp matches; we tried several in vain, before we got one to ignite. As we stopped, the rain drops from the trees beat a tattoo on our backs which felt completely unprotected. Several times, over the bumpy road, the lights went out; the tedious performance with the matches had to be gone through again. Eventually we arrived, thankful that we had escaped a puncture, to add to our discomfort. How glad we were to be in such comfortable 'digs.' After a hot bath, and a bountiful meal, the journey was forgotten.

Our time was always well filled. Dash and I produced concerts at our respective schools when most of the rehearsing with the children was done out of school time. We also helped with the various village functions, being called upon to do anything from designing posters, to washing up. Once I was asked to play the accompaniments at an assembly in the little Chapel which was opposite our former 'digs' at Hurley. I agreed, but it wasn't quite what I had expected. The instrument was a harmonium, which had seen better days. There were pedals, and also flaps at the side which were pressed out by the knees, to increase the volume. It was my first experience of such an instrument.

The address was given by an earnest young man with a nasal accent, and then the Concert began. The first item was the 'Lost Chord,' sung by a male singer with a very pleasant voice. By the time this finished, I had begun to feel more at ease with the harmonium. Next came the 'Holy City.' In the chorus, 'Jerusalem, Jerusalem, hark how the angels sing' the whole congregation joined with great fervour. Then a soprano sang a melancholy, class conscious ditty, in which a lame child of high degree bestowed a flower upon a beggar maiden. They both suffered an early death, and entered heaven side by side. Many eyes were furtively wiped after this rendering. The next offering came from a breathy singer —another sad dirge. The first two verses were in a major key, the third verse, in which the decease was related, was in the minor. As this verse started, the discord was horrible. I found the singer preferred to sing this, too, in the major and harmony was restored.

Dash had come with me, ostensibly to turn over the pages. She had parked herself upon the pulpit steps, which were immediately behind the harmonium. Here, out of sight of the congregation, she gave way to suppressed giggles. Worse was to follow. There was another short address, and then the speaker announced, 'Before our next solo, our accompanist will play an overture.' I could not believe my ears—an overture to what? I had brought no music with me, and I was very poor at memorising. I had no knowledge of what was to come, so I was afraid that what I was about to attempt, would be the opposite of an overture, but more or less a resumé of what had gone. Fortunately most of the music was still in position. I played bits of this, interspersed with fragments of 'Handel's Largo' and a bit of Chopin, finishing with the march I played for the children at school. This, I hoped sounded quite different when played Molto Andante. Never had I, nor anyone else, I hope, heard such a hotch potch. I finished with sweat standing out on my forehead. Dash was still enjoying her secret giggles. Fortunately, the rest of the evening passed without incident, and as I was warmly thanked at the end, I felt grateful for their uncritical appreciation.

Not long before the summer holiday, Betty confided that she was going to have a baby. We congratulated her as she admitted that she was pleased, but rather frightened. She begged us not to pass on the information. Pregnancy was usually kept secret until it was self evident. Then the mother-to-be kept herself away from the public gaze as much as possible. She seldom went out. No pre-natal advice was sought, or given; any small garments being made were hastily concealed at the arrival of visitors.

Betty said she had only told us because she thought we ought to find some other 'digs.' She would not be able to look after us as she had done, she said, besides feeling very embarrassed when our boy friends called. Perhaps, she said, we could find somewhere by September. We promised sadly that we would try, but we did not think we should ever be so lucky again.

We often visited the homes of the farmers who formed our dance Committee. The Ellises, who were younger than the others, and childless, made us especially welcome. We called on them, before breaking up for the holiday, and told them we were seeking new 'digs.' The fictitious reason we gave was, that we found the distance too great in the winter. As they knew everyone in Hurley, we wondered if they could suggest any possibility for us. They promised to think about it.

When Mrs Ellis went into the kitchen to make some coffee, her husband joined her. They were away some time, before he returned bearing the tray. As we supped our coffee, Mrs Ellis said 'Frank and I have been talking it over, and we wondered if you would like to come here to live.' We were surprised, and delighted. We readily agreed. Mrs Ellis, we knew, was not as good a housekeeper as Betty, but the farm house was better accommodation than we had hoped, or expected, to find in the village. It was agreed that Mr Ellis should fetch our surplus luggage, mostly books, that we were not taking home with us, from the Braithwaites. We would return to the Ellises at Heanley Farm when the schools re-opened. Dash would then have but a short walk to school; my journey would be little more than a mile and a half, which would give credence to our fictitious reason for leaving.

We said 'Goodbye' to Betty and her comfortable home with re-gret. Betty seemed genuinely sorry that we were going, but we promised to visit her often, and to do some knitting for the baby. We went for a last game of tennis the night before we left, and said 'Good-bye' to the boys, promising to see them again when we returned in a month's time. At least, that is what I promised Don. What Dash promised Howard I was to learn later, for they had sauntered off. This was a habit they had had for some time. I was always home well in advance of Dash, but this night she was later than ever. I was in bed, but I went down to let her in. Her cheeks were flushed, her eyes were shining, and she was full of excitement. 'We are engaged,' she said, 'Howard and I are engaged, but it's a secret.' I put my fingers to my lips, but she babbled on.

I could not share her excitement. In fact I felt disturbed, but mustering a smile, I said 'You must tell me all about it in the morning.' Returning to bed, I closed my eyes and feigned sleep. Sleep, however, did not come, as I thought of the arguments I could use to bring home to her the folly of this step. To me, it seemed utterly unsuitable. Per-haps I was prejudiced and he had better qualities than those I attri-buted to him. In any case, would anything I could say to Dash make any impression.

This was her first love affair, the only boy friend she had ever had, or in whom she had shown any interest. Would it be kind to throw the cold water of common sense over her idyllic mood? For some time, I had thought that she was getting too involved with Howard, but as she never told me what passed between them, it was hard to judge. I decided to say nothing to destroy her present bliss, although amazed at the object of it. She had met far more presentable boys who at first seemed attracted to her, but these had always met with a rebuff.

One of these was Harry Spare, John's friend. They often came together to Church, and the four of us would walk along the lane together. At the Valentine's Dance at Hurley, John had invited Dash and me to go with him and Harry, to the theatre in Birmingham. The arrangement was that we should go to town by train, from our nearest station, and they would meet us at Birmingham. Everything went according to plan. On the way to the theatre we passed the flower girls proffering their wares from the curb. John bought a bunch of violets which he pinned on for me. Harry asked Dash if she would like some. 'No thank you' she said, 'I never wear them.' This was said so ungraciously, that I blushed for her, but Harry showed no chagrin. Dash seemed throughout the afternoon so unlike her gay self that I was puzzled. Afterwards, I thought that she hadn't really wanted to come, but would rather have spent the time with Howard. I had not realised then, what her feelings were towards him.

# 12. *Unrequited love*

IT WAS GOOD to be with Winifred again during the holiday. Although we had written copious epistles to each other, there was a great deal to be talked over. She was greatly interested in the boy friends, and wanted to know about them in detail. How tall were they? What was the colour ot their hair and their eyes? Had I a photo of them? She posed so many questions, that I found myself scrutinising them far more closely in memory than I had ever done in reality. I wondered what sort of mental image Winifred had formed; and what the boys would have thought of the minute examination they had undergone. The enquiry was finished; the story was told, and Winifred was apparently satisfied. 'Well' she said 'Which is it to be, Don or John?' 'Probably neither,' I replied. 'Certainly not Don. He is lazy and takes no responsibility on the farm, but leaves it all to his father. He seems to have no ambition, and I really can't imagine Don exerting himself enough to keep a wife; but he's a delightful companion, and I'm very fond of him. Dancing and tennis wouldn't be the same without Don.' 'What about John' said Winifred. 'Oh, that is still on the knees of the gods, we shall have to wait and see.'

The holiday was not so happy and carefree as usual, for war clouds were gathering, and everyone was anxious. Surely war could be averted. The daily papers were read avidly, seeking any grain of comfort to be gained from the speeches of Earl Grey, or any other Statesman. Annie had not come home, but that was not unusual, for she was very fond of travel, often spending her holidays on the Continent. Sometimes she took Stanley with her. They were more

alike than Annie and I, and they enjoyed each other's company. Each
day we expected to get a post card from France or Switzerland
perhaps, with X marks the spot. Annie was very self sufficient and
told us little of her plans. At last a letter arrived, and we could tell
from the look on mother's face that the news was disturbing. Surprising, it certainly was, for Annie wrote:—

'I expect you will be very surprised to hear that I was married last
Wednesday, to Angus McNeille. You know how I hate fuss, so
Angus and I decided to have a quiet ceremony. There was no one
there, but the necessary witnesses. I wish you could have been present,
but I was afraid that if you knew, you would persuade me to have the
ceremony at home, with all the attendant worry, commotion, and
unnecessary expense. I hope it will not be long before you meet
Angus; I am sure you will like him. At present he is farming with his
father, and for the time being we shall live in a cottage on the farm.
We hope soon to have a farm of our own. After our short honeymoon, I shall be busy with our new house, then I shall return to school
until my notice expires. As you know, three months notice is
expected. When this is finished, and I have the house to my liking, I
hope that father and you will be my first visitors.' The address at the
top of the letter was of a Bournemouth Hotel, but the address of her
new home was not given.

Mother passed the letter to me, but was too distressed, at first, to
make any comment. I knew what a blow it was for her. She had
always been so proud of Annie, of her looks and her attainments.
There had always been such a friendly relationship between them.
Why, then, had she behaved like this? It was so unkind, so unfilial.

I tried to comfort mother by saying, 'Annie was always practical
and sensible, and I'm sure she would look much better in a costume,
than she would have done in a trailing bridal gown, with orange blossom. She really did save us all a lot of fuss and bother'—But I knew
the hurt had gone too deep for mere words to afford any solace.

Dash had written to me several times; from the tone of her letters
she did not appear to be very happy. Her last letter gave the reason.
She had received no communication at all from Howard since she
had been home, in spite of the fact that she had written to him. What
did I think was the reason for this complete silence. Surely Don or
someone would have let her know if Howard was ill. What could
be the matter

I wrote and told her not to worry. He was probably working hard, and trying to catch up with some of his neglected studies. Don and I had not thought of writing to each other, so I could get no information from that source.

It certainly seemed very strange behaviour, but then I had always thought of Howard as a callow, unpredictable youth. Dash never did things by halves, and she had certainly tumbled headlong into this affair. Had she I wondered been too precipitate, and might get hurt.

The holiday ended. Dash and I met on the platform at Rugby, and travelled to our new 'digs' together. I thought Dash looked thinner, and not as well as usual, but I made no comment. Mr & Mrs Ellis welcomed us at the farm, with a substantial meal. We felt that we were going to be comfortable in our new home.

As soon as we were alone together, Dash unburdened herself. She repeated what she had told me in her letter, and said that she had still had no word from Howard. She was so worried, that she had not been able to sleep. There was no one in whom she could confide, except me, as Howard had insisted that they keep their engagement secret.

It would not be long now, I said, before we went to tennis, and then everything would be cleared up. Until then, it was best not to worry. The first few evenings were dull and drizzly, but at last came a dry fine evening, when play was possible, so off we went.

The boys were already on the court, and we played as usual, until the light failed. I   new that Dash and Howard had not had a opportunity for any conversation. As soon as the last set finished, he started towards the house. Dash stood hopelessly twiddling her racket. 'Howard' I called 'Here a minute.' As he came, somewhat reluctantly I thought, Dash and Don disappeared. 'Howard,' I said 'Why didn't you answer Dash's letters? She  has been very worried, and thought you might be ill.' 'I know' he said 'I feel dreadful about it. Then he told me that as soon as we had left for the holiday, his parents had him on the carpet and told him that he was wasting his time. His employer had got in touch with them, and said that his work was careless as his mind was not on it. Unless he improved he was wasting their time, as well as his own, and would be a failure. He had been obliged to promise the firm, and his parents, that he would concentrate on his studies and work.

His mother had said that he was too young to be thinking of girls: that could come later. Then she asked if he was writing to Dash, and he had said No. So, he said, that although he had been miserable, he could see the wisdom of concentrating on his job, if he was to have any sort of future.

As I was not supposed to know of the secret engagement, I could not say all that was in my mind. I did say that he had behaved most unkindly towards Dash, and I thought he should have sent at least one letter to her, explaining the situation. He looked very young and spineless; I really felt that Dash would agree one day, that things had happened for the best.

Dash was waiting for me in the lane, and I told her what Howard had said. She passed no comment, but agreed with me, that our tennis evenings at the farm must end.

In the weeks that followed, we played several times on the hard court at the Club, but Dash seemed to have lost interest. She was despondent; quite unlike her usual self. I tried to interest her in the various activities on the farm at Heanley. She did find some amusement in watching the antics of Beardy, the goat. He was an old Billy, who had the freedom of the farmyard. Often he could be seen clambering over the lower roofs of the buildings.

When he was near the house, he proved alarming to visitors. He would run towards them with his head down in a most menacing fashion. It was his idea of fun, for he had never been known to attack anyone. Strangers were not aware of this, and would try to dodge him. This would result in a crazy game of hide and seek, round the farm carts, or anything else that provided protection. Beardy enjoyed it, and would successfully prevent any effort to escape, until someone went to the rescue. We were always amused by the ridiculous pantomime. Our mirth was perhaps unkind, for we were always careful not to get ourselves into the same predicament.

We could never understand why Mr Ellis kept Beardy, for he apparently served no good purpose. He was a continual nuisance, and had an all pervading and most obnoxious smell.

The farm was a mixed one, cereals and roots were grown, there was also a small flock of sheep, and a few cows. The cowman was known as 'Urgent' a name bestowed upon him with apt humour, by the villagers, because of his slowness. 'Urgent' was a scarecrow figure. He wore corduroy trousers tied beneath the knee with binder twine. Some of this he used in lieu of braces. His dingy shirt was collarless, his mud coloured coat had obviously belonged to a bigger man. On his head he wore a greasy old hat.

When he began to milk, he first squibbed a little over his hands. Seeing the state of his hands, which, like his clothes, were the colour of the soil, I wondered what he might be adding to the milk in the bucket.

Clean milk was not yet the concern of the Government. Three were no washing facilities, the cows were not groomed, nor was it even imagined that they could be milked by machinery.

Ever eager to learn anything new, I asked Mr Ellis if I could be shown how to milk. He readily agreed. Frank, as we soon called him, was always glad to be relieved of any job. No doubt he thought that if I became efficient, I could give a hand at busy times.

He produced a stool and said I could start on Pansy, a quiet cow and an easy milker. I soon learned to extract the milk. I should not find them all like Pansy, Frank said, for some would refuse to give down their milk except to the one to whom they were accustomed.

Getting the milk was not the only problem. To begin with, I sat with my head pressed against the side of Pansy. She soon took advantage of this, and it seemed to me that she was using my poor head as a leaning post. 'Urgent' appeared to have his head in the same position, which probably accounted for his greasy hat. Either he was indifferent to their pressure, or the other cows did not take the same advantage as Pansy.

Another hazard was the placing of the full bucket. Carelessly placed, an unexpected move on the part of Pansy would send the lot flying. This only happened once: I learnt how to avoid accidents, and how to sit without providing a prop.

Winifred came to spend a few days with us. She was very fond of milk, and it was her great delight to come to the cowshed, to have a glass of milk straight from the cow, still warm. I preferred mine when it had been strained and cooled. I always made sure that Winifred had her drink from the milk in my bucket, and not any that might have passed through the grimy hands of 'Urgent.'

# 13. Misadventure

WAR HAD BEEN declared, but as yet the announcement had made little impact on the village. We started our weekly dances again, and the Fol-de-Rols were revived. Our Concerts were popular, so we were invited to give performances in surrounding villages for Red Cross funds, and other charities. We usually made our journeys in a float, piling in all together, and jog trotting to our destination along the country lanes—strolling players with a difference.

We no longer attended our usual Church, as an encounter with Howard might prove embarrassing for Dash. Don now came to the dances alone. John was becoming a frequent visitor at the farm. He was friendly with the Ellises, whom he had known for many years; so he was usually invited to stay for a meal. John was now working for the Army in some capacity, wearing an officer's uniform in which he looked extremely smart. His job was to buy fodder for the Army horses. Sometimes I believe he actually purchased horses, or found out where they could be obtained.

John made the journeys in his father's car. Sometimes on a Saturday, he would ask Dash and me to go with him. There were few motor cars in the village; a long drive in one was a great treat. We pinned on our hats securely before setting out, lest the wind, as we flew along in the open car, should whip them from our heads.

Mrs Ellis, or Gertie, as we had been asked to call her, catered for us very well. The food was good, and ample. We would often give her a helping hand at the week-end, which she appreciated, for she was not a very competent house keeper. We were horrified to find the house was over run with mice.

Our tennis rackets, and various other things were kept in a wall cupboard in our bedroom. One day Dash found, to her dismay, that the strings of her racket had been gnawed through. Mine was intact, but a great deal of my music lay on the floor in a confetti like mess. We felt that something must be done, but we didn't like to complain to Gertie. We decided to try to deal with the destructive little pests ourselves.

From the village shop we bought half a dozen little nipper traps, and awaited our opportunity. The first evening that we had the house to ourselves, we baited the traps, and set them on the shelves in the large pantry. We were scarcely outside before we heard Click! Click! as the traps went off. We collected the corpses, and re-set the traps. The evening's effort produced a goodly 'bag,' We performed the cremation ceremony in the kitchen range.

We took the traps with us, when we went to bed, and set them at strategic points in the cupboard, and round the room. The resulting bodies were placed in a paper bag. As we scattered them on the way to school, we wondered if they would provide food for the birds.

After a few repeat performances the traps remained empty. We wrapped them up, in case they should again be necessary. We might have thought that Gertie was unaware of her small, thieving visitants, although it seemed impossible, but one day we found her in tears. In her 'best' room, that we had never yet seen used, she had found the hearthrug completely denuded of its fringe. This must have occurred before our onslaught. We were surprised that she still made no mention of dealing with the menace, so we were glad that we had taken the matter into our own hands.

The Ellises were very hospitable. Most week-ends farming friends would be invited, or would drop in casually, to an informal supper party. Dash and I usually helped with the setting and clearing away of the meal. When it was over, the men would settle to a game of 'Nap,' the wives would entertain each other with village gossip.

But Dash was still unhappy. One day she said she really couldn't endure the village any longer, it was too full of memories. She thought she would try to get a post in her own home town. If she could, she knew her mother would be pleased.

Although I knew how much I should miss her, I did not try to dissuade her, for she was so unsettled. Surprisingly, she did not have to wait long for a vacancy. There were more available at this time because many of the male teachers were joining the Forces. Dash applied, was accepted, and she left at the end of the term.

Things seemed strange without her. She was greatly missed at the Dances, and there was no one to take her place in the Fol-de-Rols. The vacancy Dash had created at Hurley school was filled by a young newly trained teacher, named Isabelle Bowen. The headmaster asked the Ellises if they would consider having Isabelle, in place of Dash. They agreed, so she became one of the family.

Isabelle was a nice girl, but different in almost every way from Dash. She came from a large town, and was quite unused to country ways. Neither dancing, nor tennis appealed to her. She played the piano well, but with accuracy rather than feeling. Knitting and crochet were her pastimes; she would much rather sit in the house, than cycle, walk, or take part in any outdoor activities.

At the first supper party after Isabelle had joined us, the conversation turned, as it often did, on the price of cattle. This talk was usually confined to men, the women might discuss the price of eggs, but were generally more concerned with domestic matters. Suddenly Isabelle joined in. 'I've been reading the "Farmer and Stock-breeder"' she said, 'I saw where a bull had been sold for a thousand pounds—A thousand pounds for a bull! Whatever good is a bull?' There was a silence for a moment, and then a great clatter of cutlery, as all became engrossed in eating.

Later I had a private conversation with Isabelle, which I hoped was informative. I advised her to take no part, in future, in the men's farming discussions.

To fill in some of the time that Dash and I would have spent together, I directed my energy towards the garden. This like many farm gardens, was sadly neglected. The men found the hand labour in a small plot most tedious after dealing with acres by an efficient machine. The kitchen garden, which had been roughly tended, produced vegetables for the house, but otherwise very little had been done. I was given a free hand, finding much pleasure in producing some sort of order, and I hoped future beauty.

John was still a frequent visitor. He would often call when he was going shepherding, as he called it, and we would walk together to inspect his cattle. We were still on formal terms, not yet had he called me by my Christian name.

During one of our walks he asked if I would like to go to the

Pantomime in Birmingham. His sister Nell and a friend would also be going: propriety would thus be observed!

I said that I should enjoy it, so he promised to let me know the date and the time.

It was arranged that he would come for me in the early afternoon. We would then pick up Nell and her friend at his home, in time to go into town for tea before the theatre.

On the appointed Saturday, I got ready with extra care. During the Christmas holidays, I had bought a new frock and coat, which I decided to wear. The frock was of brown wool with a cream Peter Pan collar, and the coat, which had cost more than I cared to remember, was of brown velour. Round the neck, was a narrow band of fur, two rows of dull round bronze buttons on the front, gave it a double breasted look. My brown woollen stockings, of course, scarcely showed, but I wore the brown shoes which were only for 'occasions.' The heels of these were higher than any of my others.

Over my small hat of brown velvet, which sported a fluffy cream feather, I wore a veil, which hung just below my nose, and which, I had been told, was quite the latest thing. Putting on my cream doeskin gloves, I came downstairs, and entered the sitting room. There was a chorus of 'Ooo's and Ah's from Isabelle and Gertie. 'My! my!' said Mr Ellis 'Dressed to kill.
They duly admired the coat and frock, and were intrigued by the veil, as I sat and waited for my escort.

Two o'clock came, and the minutes ticked on. Three o'clock came, there was still no sign of the car. It was nearly four o'clock before John came, full of apologies. The car had been giving trouble he said, and as none of the family was very knowledgable about cars, it had taken a long time to get going.

We set off, with Gertie, Isabelle, and Frank waving and laughing at the gate, to speed us on our way. John's house was a large three storied square house standing boldly on a hill.

As soon as we got to the rising ground, but still some distance from the house, the car began to splutter and complain, finally to stop. 'Oh, damn!' said John 'Now what shall we do?

After a few moments thought, he said 'I know, I'll see if Uncle Jack will lend me his car, its the same make as ours. He lives just over there' indicating a farm house, about two fields away. He was soon running along the lane leading to it, leaving me in the car.

He had no sooner gone than a drizzly rain started. Fortunately,

I had brought an umbrella. There was no hood to the car, or if there was, it had not been put up—often an exasperating and awkward job. I sat, perched on high, holding my umbrella, waiting once again.

Uncle Jack drove John back in his car. I was introduced to him, and he offered to take us the rest of the way. Then he would see if he could find the trouble in the other car. As we went, John said that as it was too late to get to town for tea, we had better have it before we went.

This I had not anticipated. I had met several members of John's family, but had not expected to be thrust among them like this without warning. Nell met us at the door. 'You have been a long time John' she said. 'Whatever happened? We've had our tea.' 'Oh' said John 'It was the blooming car again.' Nell took my wet umbrella, and we went into the house. What an ordeal! the room we entered was full of people. Besides the family there was Peter, Nell's friend, Uncle Jack's wife, Aunt Molly, and also a friend of Mrs Breedens with her two daughters.

I did not know who they all were at the time but was only conscious of countless eyes upon me, as John and I sat for a hasty tea. Fortunately, I was used to being before the eyes of a class, but they were not full of the curiosity and appraisal of those now bent upon me. I was glad when Uncle Jack came with the car, which he said was now functioning properly.

With Nell and Peter we set off again, but not all the way to town by car. There was a train we could catch at Water Orton, about two miles away, John said, that would be quicker and better, as it was still raining.

We got to Water Orton without mishap. John drove up a short hill and parked the car in a friend's yard, near the Station. We did not have long to wait for the train, so reached the theatre in good time. The Pantomime was amusing, spectacular, and we all enjoyed it.

When the Show was over we made our way to the station. Unfortunately, none of us knew that the late train left from a different platform. We waited for a while on the usual one before discovering this. As we hurried down the steps to the right platform, we saw the tail lights of our train disappearing in the distance. At first we refused to believe it. We couldn't have lost the last train—but we had. Our destination was eight miles away, what should we do?

After enquiry, we found that a train left in half an hour for Castle

Bromwich, which was in our direction, about two miles from Water Orton where we had left the car. This seemed the best we could manage and we were relieved to find even a partial solution to our problem.

We left the train at Castle Bromwich and started on the two miles walk. The first mile was uphill. The night was dark, the roads muddy. Greatly regretting my high heels, I walked with John, Nell with Peter, but we could hardly see each other in the darkness. Fortunately the rain had ceased.

When we had walked for about a mile, John stopped. Turning to me, he said 'I can't tell you how sorry I am that things have gone wrong like this' and he bent and kissed me—his first kiss—a peck on the cheek, through a damp veil.

At last we were at Water Orton. With relief we climbed into the car. John pressed the starter. Nothing happened. He pressed again and again, but there wasn't a sound. Getting out, he used the starting handle, swinging it vigorously but with no result. Then Peter had a go, he wound and wound, but there wasn't a murmur.

'There's only one thing for it' said John, 'We must push the car out and see if it will start as it runs down the hill.' We tried, but without reward. The engine remained mute, there wasn't even the slightest cough.

Here was another predicament. We would gladly have left the wretched nuisance where it was, but we daren't leave it as an obstacle in the lane; it had to be got back somehow into the yard.

Laboriously we turned it round. Then while John guided it, Peter, Nell and I pushed the monster, with all our strength. We scarcely dared pause to draw breath. The mud was no help. As we slipped and slithered, I thought regretfully of my nice brown shoes. Although the hill was only a short incline, it seemed to us steep and never ending.

Eventually we reached the top, where the car was replaced in the safety of the yard. With dismay, already exhausted, we started to walk the remaining two miles. It was two o'clock in the morning when we arrived. As it was quite impossible for me to return to Hurley, Nell invited me to share her bed, an offer which I gratefully accepted. We stumbled up the stairs at once, refusing the offer of a hot drink which the boys said they were about to make.

The family did not seem unduly surprised when I appeared at breakfast the next morning. They were used to casual visitors.

Relatives and friends often came, and stayed over night. John's father was however, dismayed when he heard of our experiences, but said he would arrange at once to have the car overhauled.

John, he said, could drive me back to Hurley after breakfast in the trap, unless I was staying for the day.

'Oh, no,' I said 'I must get back.'
There was really no urgency, but I wanted time to myself to think things out. I knew that this acceptance into John's family would have only one interpretation, for the relatives, and for any one else who heard of it. By sheer accident, the relationship between John and myself would appear to have altered. Was I ready for what this implied? I didn't know.

The Ellises, who had realised that it would be late when I returned, hadn't known that I was not home, till I didn't come to breakfast. I soon told them the tale of the car, and the reason for my absence. Gertie wanted to know what I thought of John's family, but I answered non committally, that I thought they seemed very nice.

# 14. The Proposal

THINGS WERE NOT the same without Dash. Much of the fun was gone. The things that had afforded us so much amusement, could not be shared with any one else.

Then, too, the war had thrown its shadow over the village. Everything had taken on a more sober tinge. Several of the village lads had joined up. In most of the homes, there was the click! click! of knitting needles, as khaki socks were made by the dozen.

Socials and Whist Drives were still held, the profit being given to the Red Cross, or used to buy cigarettes and comforts for the serving boys. The weekly dances, too, were carried on. These had become an embarrassment to me, for the rivalry between Don and John was a source of amusement to, and often ribald comment from, the on-lookers.

Since Dash had gone, Don had often met me, as I was on the way home from school. He came on his bicycle, offering no excuse for his presence, so far from his farm. The reason was becoming all too obvious. We only chatted about inconsequent things, but his looks told much. I was really very fond of him; I had to call upon my common sense, to prevent myself from falling in love with him. His devotion, dancing and tennis were not enough on which to base a marriage. Why! oh why! was I so conscious of his failings.

The very fact of these stolen meetings weighed against him. He should not have been there. It was really milking time, when he should have been busy on the farm. Would he always put pleasure before duty? Work never seemed important in his scheme of things.

I had never known him to refuse any outing or entertainment on a plea of work. Surely life demanded a sterner code of conduct, greater devotion to duty, and the putting of first things first.

Why was I thinking so seriously and anxiously about these things I wondered. No word of love had ever passed between Don and me, but words are not always necessary, and I had a feeling that a climax was approaching. It was a good thing that I had called common sense to my aid, for one afternoon he began by saying that he had decided to join up. He would not have been called upon to do so, even if conscription came, for he was now the only worker on the farm, and would therefore be 'reserved,' but he felt restless, and would welcome the experience.

'You know how I feel about you' he said 'But I suppose it's no good What have I got to offer? When I come back—if I do come back, I shall try for a job, as a Bailiff on an estate; but why should you think of a chap like me, when you've got better chances?'

His look was so pleading and desolate that I longed to comfort him, but what could I say? I mumbled something to the effect that we had always been such good friends, couldn't we leave it that way for the present

'I knew I hadn't a hope,' he said, and bent upon me a look of such hopeless longing, that my defences crumbled, and I was in his arms, being kissed as never before.

Coming to my senses, with flaming cheeks, I retrieved my bicycle from the hedge, and was away, no further word being spoken.

Don joined up, and I received a brief note from him, telling me where he was stationed. I wrote back, wishing him well, in a way that could only be interpreted as friendly. My conscience had troubled me, lest, dwelling on the manner of our parting, he was living on false hopes.

It may have been due to the departure of Don, that John's visits to Hurley became more frequent. He no longer pretended that he came to see the Ellises only, but he often stayed for supper and a game of cards. Sometimes I would go 'shepherding' with him. Occasionally on a Saturday, we would take a picnic lunch and I would go with him on his fodder buying expeditions. These he said, were soon coming to an end. He would then join the Army with Peter, Nell's boy friend, and Geoffrey, a cousin, who were going to join at the same time, hoping that they would be able to train, and perhaps serve together.

There were persistent rumours, that there would soon be enforced military service. John did not want to be 'conscripted.' He had wished to join earlier, but his parents had been against it. They thought that with the job he was already doing for the Army, his work on the farm, as well as that of a special constable, he was doing duty enough.

One early evening, the Ellises, Isabelle and I were sitting quietly, when there was a curious rumbling noise outside the house. The walls seemed to vibrate. We were very puzzled. 'Do you think there is something or someone prowling about' I asked Mr Ellis. 'If there is' he said 'They can jolly well stay there.'

The unusual sound continued, so with curiosity getting the better of me, I went outside to investigate. Pulsing and rumbling sounds were coming from the sky, but growing fainter. I called the others to come and listen, and we all stood, till the sound faded in the distance.

In the morning, there was great excitement in the village. It was a German Zeppelin that had passed over in the night. People thought it was the L.20. The great cigar shaped thing was flying so low, that they believed a shot from an ordinary gun would have reached it.

We were sorry we had not gone out sooner, when we might have seen, as well as heard, the menacing monster.

The day of John's departure came. It was a school day when he went, so I was not able to see him off. We had said 'Goodbye' the night before and had promised to write to each other.

Without Dash, Don and John, I felt bereft indeed. As I did not find Isabelle very companionable, my chief solace was the garden. This was now beginning to pay for the attention I lavished on it. I had persuaded Isabelle to help me with the mowing and edging of the lawn; the herbaceous border was well stocked, the trees and shrubs trimmed and neat.

When it was impossible to work outside, I busied myself with embroidering, or working crotchet for supper and afternoon tea cloths, which were to go in my 'bottom drawer.' Betweenwhiles I knitted socks, jumpers and Balaclava Helmets in the ubiquitous khaki wool.

I still did my daily stint of milking. With the many letters I had to write, I managed to fill the time. John was much given to letter writing, but Don's poor efforts were brief and infrequent. No sentiment was ever expressed, except that he concluded with 'Your devoted Don' adding crosses for kisses.

John, on the other hand, was far more amorous in his letters, than he had ever been in person.

When the time came for his first leave, to my surprise, I had a letter from Mrs Breeden asking me to spend the week-end with them while John was at home. This would be my first visit since the ill fated theatre party. At first I was undecided whether to accept or not.

It had come to my ears, by the usual village channels, that Mrs Breeden was not very pleased at the thought of her son marrying a teacher. 'Teachers,' she was quoted as saying, 'Would never make good farmers' wives. They were always gallivanting about, or had their noses in books. What did they know of housekeeping?'

It was a sweeping statement, which no doubt might apply to some. She knew little of me, and nothing of my home. No doubt she would have been most surprised had she known how carefully Mother had instructed her daughters in household chores, such as cooking, sewing and cleaning. Annie and I had helped with all, in our methodical, well run home, with the exception of washing, which was the responsibility of the washer woman, Mrs Webb, who came in for this one job, but we did assist with the mountainous pile of ironing.

Gertie Ellis was most indignant, when she heard what John's Mother had said, as Dash and I had several times prepared meals as well as helped in the house in various ways. Gertie resented the slight that had been put upon 'her teachers,' as, of course, I did myself.

I thought over the invitation. Suppose I refused. Then, I was sure, John would spend most of his time at Hurley! Would this be fair to his parents? It might not be long before he was plunged into the horror of war. The casualty lists grew longer every day, and who knew what might happen? Besides, my refusal would be sure to alienate Mrs Breeden still more, so I accepted.

John arrived home one Friday evening and fetched me early on Saturday morning. I had a warm welcome from his Father and the younger members of the family. Mrs Breeden was somewhat less expansive, but hers was not a genial nature.

The weather was fine and we had a very happy day. John and I walked round the farm in the morning; in the afternoon he drove his Mother, Nell, and me, to visit various relatives. In the evening, there was the inevitable game of cards. Besides her interminable knitting, this seemed to be Mrs Breeden's only form of relaxation. Auction Bridge had recently become popular, and a small club had been formed in the village. When this was superceded by Contract Bridge, Mrs Breeden and several friends paid frequent visits to Birmingham to learn the new rules. They carried with them, and frequently consulted, the details of what they considered the complicated scoring.

No bridge was played on this particular evening, but only round games in which everyone could join. When these finished, the family retired leaving John and me alone together. It was the first time that we had ever had the privacy of a room to ourselves. Not yet was the day of the comfortable motor car, in which one could find privacy and shelter. The only times John and I had been alone, was on our long walks together, or perched in the draughty car. Incredible as it may seem, John and I had always behaved with the utmost decorum. We had exchanged a few kisses but there had been no familiarity. Now the stage was set for I knew not what. John led me to one of the large comfortable chairs by the fire and drew me on to his knee.

When he asked if I would become engaged to him, I told him that I thought his Mother would not be very pleased if this should happen. 'What does that matter' John said 'It is my life, I shall do as I wish.' This, to me was not very reassuring, it seemed to indicate that the possibility had been discussed with disapproval. I promised to think it over. John begged me to give him an answer before he went back to Camp but this I would not promise. I still said I would think about it and let him know.

Was it imagination or did I imagine a lessening of tension on the part of Mrs Breeden next day when the relationship between John and myself remained apparently unaltered?

Each letter that came from John afterwards carried the same question. When would I give him my answer. My thoughts flew hither and thither like an imprisoned bird. The decision was so vital, the consequences so far reaching. Was I the right wife for John? Was he the right husband for me? Would this be the ideal union I had envisaged or was such perfection merely fantasy? Life seemed to be compounded of compromise.

Did everyone have to face this quandary or was I singular in this respect? Was it marriage itself at which I baulked? My lack of knowledge and the severe inhibitions against the slightest pre-marital intimacy, had made marriage seem a curious anomaly. If any natural impulse, or thirst for knowledge on the subject was unmaidenly, if such things were 'wiles of the devil,' how then could a simple ceremony transform them into 'holy' matrimony. Surely the inhibitions were too ingrained to be got rid of so readily, and a sense of guilt would remain.

It seemed such a pity that John and I were parted, when we should have been seeing more of each other, getting to know each other better. If I became engaged to John, and he went to France, the idyllic period of 'courting' which most lovers enjoyed would be lost to us. Letters would be a poor substitute, but would have to suffice.

Supposing I refused John, there would not even be letters. I imagined how John would feel if he went to war with his hopes dashed, no fond letters to send or receive. The thought was unendurable; I sat down at once, and sent him the answer he was hoping for.

John was in training on Salisbury Plain. When his next leave was about due, I suggested that when it came we should spend the weekend at my home. He welcomed the idea. It would give him the opportunity of meeting my parents and of asking my Father's consent, he said.

Such courteous conduct, I knew, would please my Mother and Father and be in direct contrast to Annie's secrecy. Sufficient time had passed, to confound the critics and to prove that the reasons she had given were the true ones.

By permission of the Managers, I had been able to have a few days off from school, and this would make it possible for me to get to London and meet John, when he arrived at Waterloo. If anything prevented our meeting there, we were to go to Victoria, where we could get the train for home, and wait there.

I got to Waterloo in plenty of time and took my stance near the platform gates. A notice declared the train to be running late. Then a further one declared that it would be running in two parts. Eventually the train arrived and from it debouched upon the platform, an incredible number of khaki clad figures. I mounted a luggage trolley, with several other people and I scanned the sea of faces, until they became featureless blurs, in a swimming mass of khaki.

The platform cleared, but there was no John. There was still a waiting crowd. The woman stanting next to me on the trolley said 'So you were unlucky too! What signal did you arrange?' When I told her that we hadn't thought of donig this she said 'Well you might as well give up, you'll never find anyone without, they all look exactly alike.' In spite of her advice, I waited for the next portion of the train.

The performance was repeated. The khaki stream flowed past me, but it was impossible to distinguish a familiar face, in that teeming throng. The crowd disappeared. There was no John and it was useless to stay any longer. I made my way to the Underground, to get a train to Victoria.

I entered the lift, the gates shut with a clatter behind me, and I looked up. There, a few steps in front of me, but facing the other way, stood John, It seemed incredible. Was I mistaken? No, I was sure, although his back was still turned towards me. 'John' I called, regardless of anyone else in the lift. He turned, and we edged our way towards each other.

John had been in the first portion of the train; had looked in vain for me. Then had decided to have a drink before going to Victoria. With the number and frequency of the lifts, it seemed a most strange coincidence, that we should happen to be in the same one.

Only Father and Mother were at home when we got there as Stanley was in the army. I could sense that my parents' first impression was favourable, and John told me that he thought they were 'jolly nice.' We were only staying at home for a couple of days, as John wanted to spend the rest of his leave at his own home.

The first day passed, and John had not found an opportunity to speak privately with Father. He said 'Your Pa is jolly elusive. He knows what's in the wind, and I don't think he is looking forward to it, any more than I am.'

At last, he managed to run Father to earth—'In the bathroom of all places'—but he refused to tell me all that had been said.

'Now that everyting is on a proper footing,' he told me jubilantly, 'I can see about the ring. What sort would you like?' My ideas were very vague. I had not given much thought to jewellery of any sort. Such aids to vanity had been severely frowned upon in my youth, so I told John I would leave it to him.

'I shan't be able to get it before I go back this time' he said, 'But I have a relation in the trade. I will get him to let you have a selection to choose from next time I come on leave. I expect that will be the one before embarkation' he said ruefully.

'Have you told your parents' I asked him. There was a pause. 'No' he said, 'But they knew I was coming home with you, so they will have guessed, and I shall tell them as soon as I get home.

When I heard this, I decided that I would not go back to his home with John as we had intended but would go straight to the 'digs.'

To be with John when he announced our engagement, would I felt be too embarrassing, no matter how the news was received. John was most disappointed, but I stuck to my decision, and he said he would come to me, the day after our return.

The Ellises seemed quite excited by my news, although they must have anticipated it, and when John came they congratulated him warmly. They told him they thought he was a very lucky fellow, and sang my praises. I felt that they were doing this, to rebut the adverse criticisms that his Mother had circulated about teachers as wives.

Winifred had met John while we were home and had heard our news first hand, but Dash had to be told by letter. Her reply was a very lengthy one. After the congratulations, she said how dull her life seemed to be and she wondered if we could get together again. When John went, she wrote, there would be nothing to keep me at Hurley. We could please ourselves where we went, so we could look for two suitable vacancies anywhere.

The more I thought about her idea, the better it pleased me. Life for me, too, would be dull when John had gone, and a change of scene might help. Then too, I was uneasy at the thought of meeting Don. So far he had not been home on leave but when he did come, a meeting would be inevitable. I shirked telling him of my engagement, but it would have to be done. I knew it would hurt him but, like the Ellises, he must have anticipated it. The news would probably put an end to our sporadic correspondence, so if I left Hurley, this sentimental episode would be closed.

I wrote to Dash, told her that I welcomed the idea of a change, and suggested that we should start scanning the advertisements at once.

This we did. It was not long before we found what we wanted. Many vacancies were occurring, as male teachers were still joining the forces. We sent in applications to two places, one near London, the other an industrial town in Warwickshire, not very far from Hurley. I was asked for interview to both places, but Dash only to the one in Warwickshire, so it was here, to Coventry, that we decided to go.

Both the positions were in Boys' Schools, but they were at opposite ends of the town; we were interviewed and duly appointed.

It was while all this was taking place that John had his embarkation leave, and I spent his last week-end with him at his home. The family had become used to the idea of our engagement, and Mrs Breeden had evidently accepted it without any demur. They gave me quite a warm welcome. Mr Breeden kissed me—there was no kiss from Mrs Breeden—and made quite a nice little speech congratulating us both.

John had the selection of rings for me to choose from. We tried to find a quiet spot where we could make the choice, but it was a wet day, the family seemed to be in possession everywhere. Fortunately we found the kitchen empty in the afternoon, so in the seclusion of the back stairs, the rings were one by one tried on, and viewed. I chose one with two diamonds.

It was the least expensive, John said, but it pleased me, and when the family assembled for tea, I showed them my treasure.

John took me back on Sunday evening and we said our goodbyes. The future was so uncertain that we hardly dared to make any plans. We were not even sure when our next meeting would take place. We promised to write as frequently as we possibly could and we bolstered up each other by saying that the war could not possibly last much longer.

With heavy hearts and a feeling of utter despondency we parted.

# 15. War and Tragedy

I WAS VERY glad that I had the business of moving to Coventry to occupy my mind. There was the usual month's notice to give at school, the farewell visits to be paid.

Dash and I had kept our promise to Betty Braithwaite; we had knitted many small garments for her. When I went to say 'Goodbye' it was pleasant to see that some of these were being worn by her bonny new son. She said how pleased she was to hear of my engagement to John. 'So much better than Don' she said 'And you know, I believe I had a small part in bringing it about.' Betty was evidently referring to the time when she had unexpectedly invited John and his friend in, on the occasion of our first walk together.

It was with very mixed feelings that I said 'Farewell' to the people and places, where I had spent such a happy time.

Mrs Ellis had some friends living in Coventry. When it was settled that I was going there, she wrote to them and asked if they knew of any suitable 'digs' for Dash and myself. It was a great relief when we heard that some had been found. We knew that Coventry had received a great influx of munition workers and 'digs' were at a premium.

I was able to get to Coventry the evening before Dash's arrival. Mrs Long, the friend of Gertie, met me at the station and accompanied me to our new 'digs.' I was introduced to the landlady, Mrs Towner, and shown our bedroom and sitting room. This was quite a pleasant room at the back of the house, with a window looking over the garden.

Next morning, Mrs Long and I started early on our bicycles and
went first to the school where Dash was to teach. It was much bigger
than the little rural school at Hurley. Then we crossed the town to
the school which was to be mine. How glad I was to be shown the
way, for I should have had great difficulty in finding it. My bump of
direction was small; I had no knowledge of the outskirts of Coventry,
although I had visited the town itself on several occasions.

Mrs Long left me, and I viewed the school with surprise. It was
many times bigger than the new school at Woodend in which I had
taught.

I entered and introduced myself to the headmaster. My duties
did not start till the next day, so I was shown round and introduced
to the Staff. There were over five hundred boys in the school I was
told, wh ch seemed an enormous number to me. There were also
Girls and Infants Departments, which accounted for the size of the
buildings. On the staff of the Boys' School there was only one woman
teacher besides myself. The Head had been reluctant to have any
women, but had been compelled to do so, when there were not
enough men to fill the vacancies.

I was shown the class for which I should be responsible. It looked
to me like a whole school. There were about sixty boys, apparently
about ten years old. 'How many are there' I asked. There were sixty
four names on the register, but with absentees, the number present
was usually below that figure.

I contrasted these rough looking urchins, with my rural juniors
and began to think that I was going to have a tough job.

My Headmaster evidently had a poor opinion of women teachers
as disciplinarians, for he at once told me that at the slightest sign of
trouble I was to send for him. I hoped that such a confession of failure
on my part would be unnecessary, but I kept this to myself. I learnt
later that my class had a reputation for being unruly. Their previous
master, I heard, had been too fond of 'looking upon the wine when
it was red' and stronger beverages also. Whether it was due to this
indulgence, or for some other reason, he often arrived at school in a
vile temper, which he vented on the boys.

Be that as it may, I found the boys quite amenable in the first difficult days, which certainly surprised me. I hoped it was my influence,
but it may have been due to the near presence of the Headmaster,
who was often at his desk on the other side of the glass partition.

One thing certainly bothered me. The room was so long and

narrow that I could not get far enough back to be able to see all the class at one time.

This was not to be my permanent class. Examinations were about to begin and after them there would be an alteration. Then I was to have the youngest boys, some of whom were new comers from the Infant School.

For the examination each class teacher set the questions, which had to be vetted by the Headmaster. So, almost at once, I had to produce a set of test questions on subjects which someone else had taught. The syllabus had to be digested and I don't think I had ever had to do such intensive homework. How thankful I was when the submitted questionaire was approved.

The Head was a stern task master. He permitted no slacking and kept us all at full stretch, but he was just, and we respected him. Tall and dark, in the early fifties, he still had the figure of an athlete. When young, he had been a keen rugger player. His commanding presence, with its look of concealed strength acted as a deterrent to bad behaviour. He meted out adequate punishment when it was needed and the discipline throughout the school was excellent.

When the boys assembled in the morning, they stood in lines in the playground, according to their classes. The Headmaster himself, inspected each line, giving particular attention to shoes  hands and hair. Woe betide any boy who fell short of his standard.

Some of the lads came from very poor homes. One morning I noticed a peculiar silvery shine on the boots of one small boy. On enquiry I found that his mother had no blacking that day, but as his boots had to be cleaned, he had used black lead.

When the inspection was over, a favoured boy beat a tattoo on a drum and to this martial music they filed into school.

My usual dress for school was a tweed suit and a blouse with which I wore a tie. One day Dash and I had received an invitation out for tea and to spend the evening. As I should not have time to go back to the 'digs' after school, I had changed at lunch time into a dull red velvet frock.

During the afternoon break, I was busy at my desk when I heard the classroom door open. I looked up, but there was no one there. In a few minutes, I heard the same sound and looking up quickly I saw Tommy Chinn, one of my scholars, standing there with a boy from another class.

Tommy had a wide face, with large rather protuberant eyes and

a big mouth, In spite of his frog like appearance, he was an endearing small boy.
"Come here, Tommy' I said 'Did you open the door before?'
'Yes miss' he said.
'You know quite well, Tommy, that you are not allowed in the classroom at play time.'
'Yes miss' was the reply.
'Why then did you come in?' I asked.
'Please miss, I wanted Billy Smith to see your frock'
'Is that Billy Smith with you?'
'No, miss, this is Charlie Dodd.'

I wondered how many more he would have brought if he hadn't been discovered; and felt very touched to think that he wanted to share his own pleasure in such an unusual splash of colour. They were dismissed with a very gentle reprimand.

One of the lessons that the boys enjoyed was singing. According to my Syllabus my class was to learn Brahms Cradle Song and two similar ones. Charming though they were, I did not feel that they had much appeal for these robustious youngsters. As soon as they were well and truly learnt, we turned our attention to sea shanties and ballads. The boys appetite for these was insatiable. I'm sure they thought that the exercises, and all that had gone before, was well worth while if it led to these delightful ditties.


Our landlady, Mrs Towner, had a daughter Mabel, a little younger than Dash or I. She was short and slim, with ash blonde hair and grey eyes. Her chin was pointed and she had a small attractive face. Mabel worked in one of the large factories in the town. She seemed to have a surprising number of gentlemen friends, who called to take her out.

Mrs Towner had told us several times what a wonderful singing voice Mabel had. One day in reply to this oft repeated remark, Dash and I said we would like to hear her. 'Oh' said Mrs Towner, 'Unfortunately, she doesn't play, and there is no one to accompany her.'
'Edith could' said Dash.
Mrs Towner was overjoyed and took us into her drawing room, a holy of holies, into which we had not before penetrated. The piano was in tune and I tried over some of the songs which lay upon it. If we were not busy, Mabel would sing for us that very evening, said her mother. To this we agreed and to our surprise, Mrs Towner's opinion was fully justified. Mabel had a full rich contralto voice,

beautifully produced, although she had had no training.

Several evenings were passed very pleasantly, as Mabel went through her repertoire. Then she introduced us to Hugh Bigham, a violinist, who was on the Staff of the factory where she worked. We soon began a series of musical evenings. I played the piano, Hugh the violin, and Mabel sang. Dash sat with her crotchet or knitting, and enjoyed the entertainment.

Hugh had a brother Jim, who was in the Air Force. While he was home on leave Mabel, Dash and I were invited to their home to entertain the family with our Trio. Mabel was in good form, and sang her sentimental ballads with great feeling. We could see that Jim was impressed, and we were not surprised when he offered to join Hugh in seeing us home. He and Mabel were soon well ahead, while Hugh, Dash and I, followed behind.

Next day, a Saturday, Jim called to see Mabel almost before she had finished her breakfast. There was no music that evening, as Jim had taken Mabel out. For the remainder of his leave, Jim was a constant visitor. It was inevitable that he should clash occasionally with the visits of her other admirers, but Mabel seemed to cope with the situation, and we noticed that Jim was always the favoured one.

Jim's leave ended, and Mabel gave us the surprising news that she and Jim were engaged and would be married when he had his next leave. Hasty weddings were not unusual at this stage of the war, but we thought this had been a particularly brisk affair. Was it love at first sight on the part of Jim? or had Mabel some secret allure that was hidden from us.

Hugh said his parents were most displeased at the news and blamed him. Poor Hugh! we knew that he was quite innocent of aiding and abetting either Mabel or Jim. The whole affair had been as much a surprise to him as to any one.

Jim was the youngest of the family and the pride and joy of his mother. He was tall, handsome, with dark auburn hair which was inclined to curl and twinkling blue eyes. Full of fun, he had a store of humorous anecdotes, which he told with great gusto and enjoyed as much as anyone.

His appearance was a complete contrast to that of Hugh, who was tall, thin, and pale. He had been excused military service on medical grounds. Jim said that when sharing a bedroom with Hugh, he sometimes missed seeing him and found that Hugh was hidden by the bed post.

Mabel began her wedding preparations at once. Jim's leave came and the wedding took place. The Bighams were still very upset, and refused to attend the ceremony. Hugh came with his sister, against their parents' wishes and Dash and I were among the few guests.

The bride's gown was of white satin, with a small train. She had a wreath of orange blossom, and was enveloped in a long veil of white tulle. There were three small attendants, and her bouquet was of white lillies. Jim wore his blue Air Force uniform, as did his best man.

Although Jim was his usual merry self, there was an air of constraint at the reception. Naturally all war weddings of service men, had an undertone of sadness and anxiety as to the future. At this one in particular, there seemed a sense of foreboding. Was it an omen of things to come.?

They had a brief honeymoon before Mabel came home, and Jim returned to duty. Impatient at the delay before his next leave and longing to be with his bride, Jim took a risk.

On an authorised flight, he deviated from the scheduled course, and flew to Coventry. All might have been well if engine trouble hadn't developed. He landed safely near the town, and having pals in one of the aeroplane factories he contacted them. With their assistance, he was able to get the fault remedied as far as possible, in the short time that was allowed. Jim paid a fleeting visit to Mabel and then again took off in the plane. Something, however, was still amiss, for, on the way back, he crashed and was killed.

A few short weeks after his wedding, Dash and I attended Jim's funeral. To have lost his young life in such circumstances seemed particularly tragic. As the bearers in their Air Force blue uniforms paced their melancholy way to the grave, it was hard to believe that they carried the mortal remains of the merry boy who had been so full of joie de vivre.

Unfortunately news of other young lives being lost was all too frequent at this time. The telegrams bearing the ominous news were usually delivered in the evening. The sight of the telegraph boys hastening on their bicycles to deliver the sad news, was most depressing. As we heard the rat-tat-tat! on the knockers, our hearts went out in sympathy to the recipients of the messages, and I uttered a little prayer of thankfulness that John's life had so far been preserved.

War news became more and more gloomy. The end of hostilities, for which we all fervently hoped, seemed as far off as ever. As the winter of this unhappy year of 1917 approached, the weather was worse than usual, and the rain seemed incessant. John's letters spoke of rivers of mud in France. He was with a horse regiment, and sometimes, he wrote, the horses would become so engulfed, that it was impossible to extricate them. They had no alternative but to shoot the poor creatures. The men were spending long hours in the trenches, which were over-run by vermin. It was not only rats that bothered them. Their energies were taken up in keeping their bodies and clothes free from loathsome pests. Poor John, I thought, always so fastidious in private life, now having to devise means of ridding himself of lice. Running a lighted candle along the seams of his underwear dealt with some of the blighters, he wrote.

He was feeling most depressed at the mounting number of casualties. One of his two friends, who had joined when he did, had been killed, and the other one was severely wounded. John felt that he, himself, had been extremely lucky to have escaped. He was hoping that it would not be long now before he had leave. When I come home, John wrote, I should like us to be married. It is no use waiting for the end of the war, as we had planned, who knows how long that will be? My own end may come first.

This was the most unhappy letter I had ever received from him. The only way in which I could raise his spirits was to write at once and tell him that it should be as he wished, and our wedding should take place when he returned.

# 16. Wedding

SINCE JIM'S death the music sessions with Mabel and Hugh had ceased. This gave me more time to devote to my trousseau, which I was making by hand. Fashion in underclothes had changed, and finer and more delicate materials were used. It was no longer considered necessary to make at least half a dozen of each garment of the same shape and material. One of the numerous articles of Mother's trousseau still survived, although it had been outmoded and unworn for years. This was a calico chemise, the front of which was trimmed with fine tucks and feather stitching.

Among the innovations which had taken place in the realm of lingerie were two which Dash and I greatly liked. One was the camisole. This had superceded the bodice as a corset cover, and had shoulder straps in lieu of sleeves. The straps were often made of slotted insertion which also edged the top of the camisole. Through this, pink or blue ribbon could be threaded, and when a blouse of voile or other thin material was worn, the ribbon showed through. We thought this was very alluring, but perhaps a little immodest. Cami-knickers, as their name implied, combined two garments. Recently introduced, they were quite unlike anything we had worn before. Dash and I made ourselves some of these dainty garments in pink crepe-de-chine, to wear on special occasions. The weather was cold, and we felt that flimsy cami-knickers would be, at present, a chilly substitute for our woolly combs, and cosy knickers, which had elastic at the waist and knees.

Christmas was not many weeks ahead. I thought it would be wise to do the shopping for my wedding, before we broke up for the holiday. Coventry would offer a better choice than my little home town of Lewes. I had not yet decided what to wear on the great day. Mine would be a quiet wedding, and John would be in khaki. I wondered if a suit would perhaps be a more sensible choice, than a bridal gown and veil. However, Mother, Winifred and Dash, when consulted, all agreed that white it must be.

Many war brides-to-be were superstititous about buying their wedding dress before their fiancés came home. Some gowns alas had been bought and never worn. The dreaded telegram had arrived in lieu of bridegroom. Pushing into the background any misgivings I had, Dash and I went shopping. The gown I bought was of cream crépe-de-chine, with a georgette collar, and long sleeves. The style was plain, but the material had a faint pattern in self colour. Some cream silk stockings, and net for my veil, I bought at the same time.

When we arrived back at the 'digs' Mrs Towner, the landlady, and Mabel begged to see our purchases. When Mabel saw the dress she exclaimed 'Ooh! you must borrow my shoes, they will match exactly'. She quoted 'Something old, and something new, something borrowed and something blue.' When I remembered the sequel to the first occasion when the shoes had been worn, I felt a little tremor of dismay. If I refused it would be difficult to tell Mabel the reason, so I reluctantly accepted her offer. They were very pretty shoes of gold brocade, and I knew that Mabel and I took the same size. She went immediately to fetch them. They fitted and were comfortable.

For going away after the wedding, I decided to have a tailor made suit. Dash and I no longer went to Annie's tailor, as we had found a good one in Coventry. The material I chose was what the tailor called 'gentlemen's suiting' in navy blue, and he promised to make it quickly. To wear with it, I bought a red felt hat with a wide brim, and some doeskin gloves.

Small white fur necklets were very fashionable. Some were made of rabbit. The nicest ones were of ermine, and were naturally much more expensive. One of these, I thought, would really put the finishing touch to my outfit. Funds were getting low. The rabbit collars were much less money, but really there was no comparison, and when I remembered how easily the rabbit hairs were shed, I decided to be extravagant, and chose the ermine.

After this orgy of spending, it was necessary to take a close look at the money situation and find out what was left in the exchequer.

My wedding gift to John was to be a watch. The one he had taken with him had soon ceased to function. I had chosen, but not yet paid for, one which was guaranteed to be shock proof and water proof, which I hoped would withstand the rigours of army life.

When I had totalled up all that I owed, I found to my joy, that I should still have a small surplus in the Post Office. My War Savings Certificates I wished to keep intact, if possible. Dash was told the good news, and she agreed that it would now be possible to add an afternoon frock to my wedding ensemble.

Once more we gaily set out on a shopping expedition, to seek a pretty frock, of a kind we rarely wore. Blouses and skirts were our usual garb, with evening dresses for dances, and cotton frocks for the summer holidays. Most week-ends were spent cycling or tennis playing. Since the musical evenings ended, I had joined the local Operatic Society, and was also having organ lessons, while Dash was attending a dressmaking class; so there was little occasion to wear the type of frock which we now sought.

First of all we made our way to the largest drapery store in town, where we knew that we should find a good selection. There was nothing here, however, that pleased us sufficiently. The assistant was most pressing, and persuasive, in her efforts to make a sale, and we were really glad when we were able to escape without being cajoled into making a purchase against our wishes. After this experience we decided to so some window shopping. There were several small gown shops. Some of these carried only a limited stock, of expensive but well chosen garments. In one of these we saw a dream of a dress. It had pride of place in the window, among the few others displayed, and it glowed, literally glowed. It was of shot taffeta, tan, with a glint of blue, an autumn wood in terms of material. I was entranced, but there was no price tag visible. Would it be beyond my purse? Quite nice dresses could be bought for thirty nine and elevenpence, but not ones such as this.

'How much do you think it will be' I asked Dash, but neither of us had any idea. 'I can only afford about three pounds' I said. We entered the shop, and I enquired the price. When told that it was three and a half guineas, I hastened to try it on. The fit was perfect, and the purchase was soon made.

As far as possible my preparations were complete. I had obtained permission from the Education Committee for leave of absence when John should arrive. Mother had been warned that she would have very little notice before the wedding. Now all we could do was to wait patiently, hoping and praying, as always, that John would be preserved from the 'perils and dangers' of his hazardous life.

One day in December I cycled back to the 'digs' as usual for my midday meal. Although I knew that John would arrive without warning, it was with surprise and delight, that I found him there awaiting me. He had arrived at home late the previous evening, and had borrowed his father's car to come to Coventry. After lunch he took me back to school to break the news of my impending absence. I introduced John to the Headmaster, after which we made our way to the local Register Office. As the date of a war wedding, and even the possibility of the wedding itself, was unpredictable it was impossible to have the banns read in the usual way. Special licences, however, could be obtained, at less cost than the ones generally supplied by the Archbishop, but notice of the wedding had to hang in the office of the Registrar.

Having dealt with these formalities, we found that the earliest date for our wedding would be the following Monday. A telegram was sent to my home which read 'Home Sunday, married Monday.' Most of my clothes had been carefully packed in readiness for the hasty departure. It did not take long to pack those for immediate use, and John and I were soon on the way to his home.

Here, preparation had to be made for the journey to my home town of Lewes, nearly two hundred miles away in the South of the country. We should have to travel by train. War time rail travel was slow and difficult. Because of this, few of John's friends and relations would be able to attend the ceremony. It was decided that only Mr and Mrs Breeden, and Stafford, John's brother, would make the journey. Stafford was to be best man.

Sunday, the day on which we were to travel was cloudy and dark. Before we set off the snow began to fall. I remarked cheerfully that it would probably be fine at Lewes, as we had very little snow there. Unfortunately, the snow fall increased, and when we raeched London where we had to change stations, it lay in a thick carpet. We went by taxi from Paddington to Victoria, where we had a long time to wait. The waiting room was cold, and so was the train when it came. The pushing and jostling crowd on the platform, many of whom were soldiers, was so dense, that we wondered if we should all find room. However, we were lucky, and managed to find seats together.

Opposite us in the carriage were two women with three small children, including a baby in long clothes. One of the women, who was smartly dressed, held a child about two years old on her lap, and the other small child sat between the two adults. The woman with the young baby had a very odd appearance. She was dressed entirely in black. Although narrow skirts were now being worn, hers were still voluminous. In spite of the wintry weather, she wore a large black straw hat, and seemed distraught. Apart from the fact that they were both wearing mourning, the two women were utterly dissimilar, it seemed a strange companionship.

Judge our surprise, when, just as the train was about to start, the smart woman rose, dumped the child upon the seat, kissed her companion, and saying 'Try not to fret' left the train.

The child looked so forlorn perched precariously on the edge of the seat, that I asked the mother if I could hold her. She nodded and I gathered the little one into my arms. Suddenly, the train gave a lurch, and the other small child almost tumbled. The passenger next to me took pity, and picked that one up also. Both the children received our attentions with apathy.

Soon we became aware of a strange continuous sobbing issuing from the baby in the long clothes. Noticing our curious glances in its direction the mother suddenly spoke. 'He never stops' she said. Then she told us that she had been pregnant with this baby, when she heard the news that her soldier husband had been killed. The baby had made this unhappy sound ever since his birth, due she thought, to her continuous weeping after she had received the sad news. For some years she had lived in Ireland, and the shock of her husband's death, and having to cope with the three young children, had driven her nearly crazy. She said she was now on the way home to her mother in Lewes, having spent the night in London with her sister-in-law, the one who had helped her on the train. The baby should have been put into shorter garments weeks before, but it was so puny and miserable, that she felt it was better to keep to the long clothes. Her mother was not expecting her, but she felt that if she stayed in Ireland much longer, she would have gone completely out of her mind. From her distressed condition we thought this not at all unlikely.

We had completed about half our journey when we had to change trains. With the great demand that the army made on the train service, 'through' trains had ceased to exist for civilian use. The little family was helped on to the platform, and then Stafford and John went to retrieve the pram which, the mother said, was in the guard's van. Snow was still falling, and it was fortunate that we did not have long to wait, for there was no waiting room on the platform.

For the rest of the journey, Mrs Breeden and I each held one of the small children. At last we reached Lewes. The mother, John and Stafford went once more for the pram and luggage, Mrs Breeden held the baby, and I had a toddler in each hand, as my Father came forward to meet us.

His surprise can be imagined, at seeing the bride elect arrive with numerous progeny. He looked from me to Mrs Breeden, and then with a most quizzical expression he asked "Which is the mother?" We soon explained the situation. Father had hired one of the few taxis in the town. This was waiting for us, but we did not feel that we could leave the poor mother stranded. She seemed quite unable to cope by herself. Contrary to my forecast, the snow was falling here also, and was already becoming deep. Father found a solution to the problem. He arranged for an outside porter to take the pram and her luggage to the woman's address. She, and the babies, John's Mother and I would go in the taxi. Fortunately, the stranger lived in the same direction as our house. We delivered her safely, hoping that in the comfort of her mother's home, she might be restored to health and sanity.

The men, who had walked from the station, arrived home almost as soon as we did. Introductions were made to the family, and to Winifred and Olive, who were at home to greet us, and we were soon all seated round a bountiful and welcome meal. Tongues were soon wagging and any stiffness disappeared.

It had been arranged that Winifred should spend the night with me. John's Father and Mother would also stay with us, but John and Stafford would be accommodated at the home of Winifred and Olive.

On Monday morning I looked anxiously at the weather. The snow had stopped falling, but the ground was still covered by an unsullied carpet of white. The sky was blue and when the sun came out, the snow sparkled as if bestrewn with diamonds. I thought nature had been most kind in providing us with such a radiant wedding day.

As we sat at breakfast we could hear the sounds of activity in the kitchen. Mrs Purcell, who came to help mother on special occasions, had already arrived. She, and Betty the maid, were hard at work.

As Christmas was so near, Mother had decided that the wedding breakfast, which was to be held at home, should consist of festive fare. Turkey, Christmas pudding, and mince pies, were to be on the menu.

In the middle of the morning, the flowers arrived, and were greeted with cries of admiration. My shower bouquet was of auratum lilies and lilies of the valley, interspersed with trails of smilax. Winifred, as bridesmaid, had a posy of lilies of the valley. The Mothers each had a charming corsage, and the men a white carnation. Father put his at once into a small water container, which was fixed to the back of his coat lapel. This small gadget would retain the freshness of a flower, even when worn in a heated room. Father was fond of a buttonhole and often wore one, as did many other men. A photo of the much publicised politician, Joey Chamberlain would have looked odd, without the inevitable orchid which he wore.

The ceremony was to be at noon, and soon every one was busy getting ready. While we were so engaged, John came to borrow a white handkerchief from his Father. I was told later that when Betty, the little maid, saw him she raised her hands in horror. "Oh Sir" she said "You mustn't see the bride before the wedding. That would be terribly unlucky." John was soon away again, and Betty must have felt relief that no unfortunate meeting had occurred.

I thought Winifred looked very pretty in her bridesmaid's frock. It was of pale blue cashmere. Her hair was fair, and excitement had put some colour into her cheeks, which were usually pale. She helped me to adjust my veil. On my hair I wore a small wreath of artificial orange blossom to which the veil was secured. It would cover my face until the ceremony was over. Then it would be thrown back. What, I wondered, was the origin of this curious rite. Was it to conceal the blushes of the modest bride, or had it some other significance, of which we were not aware?

The hired cabs arrived, and all set out, with the exception of Father and myself. A little time elapsed before we started, and then we did not go by the short route past the frightening 'White Lion" of my childhood, but took the longer way round. We had judged the time to a nicety, for, as we neared the town clock, it began to strike twelve in its familiar leisurely way.

Snow had been cleared from the approach to the Church and a red carpet laid. The sun was now quite warm and the snow on the roof was beginning to thaw. At our approach I saw the caretaker hurriedly sweep from our path, a freshly fallen dollop of snow. Just as we reached the porch, another dollop fell, fortunately missing us by inches. A cold and clammy shower bath would certainly not have enhanced the proceedings.

I felt strangely nervous, and clutched Father's arm quite tightly as we walked up the aisle to where John was waiting. There was quite a large congregation. News of the hasty wedding must have spread quickly.

In his address, the minister spoke of the difference between a normal peace time wedding, when the home and future could be planned, and one which took place with war at its height. Instead of security, there was danger, instead of peace, anxiety, and instead of companionship, a parting of unknown duration. Mother told me later that there were few dry eyes among those that listened. For myself, I was in a trance, and went through the service like an automaton.

Our brief honeymoon was to be spent at Matlock, in an hotel kept by a relative. A taxi had been ordered, for four o'clock, to take us to the station. As we chatted after our meal, Mother said she thought it was a pity we were taking such a long journey for so short a time. John had done a lot of travelling in the last few days, and now that we were in the pleasant South country, why not stay somewhere near? Everyone thought this would be a good idea—how mistaken they all were—. Eastbourne was suggested, and trains were looked up. There was one just after five o'clock, so when the taxi came, the driver was asked to return in an hour. The train was late and when it arrived at the station, it appeared to be full. In spite of all John's efforts, we were unable to get a carriage to ourselves.

We arrived at Eastbourne to find the steets in almost total darkness and we had no accommodation booked. I had been to Eastbourne several times, but always in the summer. Then, it had seemed gay. Bright awnings hung from the hotels. The carpet beds in the lawns on the Front were brilliant with flowers, and the multi coloured garments of the milling crowds made a kaleidoscope of colour. Now, the town was dark and quiet, with an eerie stillness.

We made our way to the Front. Fortunately, our luggage was light. We had not been quick enough to get one of the few taxis at the station, and of course, we should have had no address to give. The Front was, if possible, darker than the rest of the streets. Our footsteps echoed on the pavements, which had been cleared of snow: the drag of the shingle, as the waves ebbed and flowed, sounded melancholy and sinister.

We managed to locate an hotel, and John enquired about accommodation. Alas! it was completely full. When John asked the receptionist if she could recommend anywhere else, it was only to be told that all the hotels were also full. Most of the available accomomdation had been taken up by people from London, who were taking refuge here, to escape the bombing.

Now, what were we to do? How I wished that we had never left home, or had gone to Matlock as arranged, where we should have been sure of a resting place and a welcome. We left the Front and retraced our steps towards the station. What we intended, I do not know, but suddenly a door opened shedding a welcome glow of light. It looked like a private hotel. We flew up the steps, and almost before the door closed, beat a tattoo upon it. It was re-opened by a pleasant faced woman, but when she heard our request, it was answered in the negative. There was no room available. She was however sympathetic, and realized our predicament. "I wish I could tell you of somewhere" she said "But the town is completely full." Then after a moment's thought she told us that some people had left that morning from the private hotel opposite. "Of course," she said, "I do not know if any others have taken their place. Anyway it is worth trying. You can tell Mrs Heape, the proprietress, that I have sent you. My name is Cooper." We thanked her warmly for this ray of hope.

We made our way at once across the street to the house she had indicated. Only a faint glimmer of light showed that it was occupied. John rang the bell, and a smart middle aged woman opened the door. "Mrs Heape" said John "Yes" she replied. "Come inside". The door was quickly closed to obscure the light. We were most relieved to find that she could accommodate us for our short stay. When we had entered our names in the visitors book with all the necessary war time details, we were shown to our room. It was at the top of the four storied house and struck us as very cold. In our anxiety we had not noticed how frosty the weather had become. John put a shilling into the meter of the gas fire, but we had not time to appreciate its warmth, for we had barely removed our coats, before the gong sounded for dinner.

We had only had a cup of tea since mid-day, and realized that we were hungry. Down the many stairs we went, until we reached the basement dining room. At the long tables the other guests were already seated, and curious glances followed us as we took our places. The company was composed of young married women, some of them with children, middle aged matrons, grandmothers, and one or two elderly men. There was only one other young man, a soldier, who had with him a young wife. Possibly they too, were on their honeymoon.

All seemed very friendly together, and there was a great buzz of conversation. Many of them had been with Mrs Heape for months, and were well known to each other. They welcomed us, and said that they were making up a party for the Cinema that evening, and would we like to join them.

We had certainly not anticipated spending this particular evening with a crowd of unknown people, but, as both of us were very self conscious about our newly wedded state, we found it difficult to find an excuse, so we joined the Party.

On our return, as I was about to make my way upstairs, John whispered "I will join you in a few minutes." This pleased me, as I thought I could then undress and prepare for bed in privacy. The thought of undressing before male eyes, even if the eyes were those of my husband, I found most disconcerting. The bedroom fire had petered out, so I put in another shilling and began to undress. I took off my coat and skirt, and hung them in the wardrobe. Then I went to the case for my night things, which we had not had time to unpack.

The case was locked, and John had the key. What should I do? Should I dress again, and go downstairs to get it? John had said he would be up in a few minutes, so I had better wait. I put on my top coat, drew a chair up to the fire, and waited, and waited.

The minutes ticked by and still he didn't come. What could have happened? Once again I wondered whether to go and look for him. The absurdity of the situation suddenly struck me. One had always thought of a honeymoon as the epitome of happiness. What rosy, but erroneous pictures imagination is apt to paint. Here I sat, a bride of a few hours, no fond and eager bridegroom by my side, but alone in a cold, strange room.

At last John came, apologetic and repentant. He had gone, he said, into the drawing room for a last cigarette before coming up. As he stood by the fire, Mrs Heape had asked him if he played Bridge.

Unaware of the consequences, he had told her that he was very fond of the game and played a lot. "How lucky" said Mrs Heape, "You can make up the four, we love a rubber before we go to bed." Two players were already seated at the card table. They looked at him in eager anticipation. Mrs Heape seated herself, and motioned John to the empty chair. He had found it impossible to extricate himself. Of course John had not remembered that the keys to the suitcases were in his pocket. I made no comment. My mood had changed. The ardent excitement which had been with me all day, had slowly evaporated. During my lonely vigil I had descended from the Cloud Cuckoo Land of my imagination, to the plane of reality, and realized that I was cold, tired and disappointed. It was in this subdued frame of mind that I entered the nuptial bed to discover, not without discomfort, the mystery which had for so long perplexed me.

In the morning the window was covered with beautiful fern patterns made by the frost. The day was bright, and when the sun came out after breakfast, we decided to go for a walk. We climbed to the top of Beachy Head. The snow was crisp and glistening, and apart from a few bird prints, and our foormarks, it lay in pristine freshness. When we came down from the hill, we found a sheltered seat on the Promenade where it was warm enough for us to sit for a short time in the sun. Among the foliage on the near-by bank some trails of small crimson leaved ivy were growing, and John and I each gathered some, to keep as a memento.

Our brief visit to Eastbourne soon came to an end. When we said our Goodbyes to Mrs Heape, she said, "If only you had told me, you should have had the best room in the hotel." We wondered how that would have been possible, without dispossessing some unwilling guest. She did not tell us how she had discovered our secret. Possibly in spite of our efforts to remove it, some tell tale confetti had given us away.

We started early on the day of our return, for we knew that the journey would be a tedious one. The train was slow, and we had to make two changes on our way to London. Here, we ate the sandwiches with which Mrs Heape had kindly provided us. With difficulty, John managed to get us a cup of coffee. As usual, the stations were crowded. Soldiers were everywhere, and we were jostled and pushed as we made our way to the Underground train for Euston. It was quite impossible to get either a porter, or a taxi. We were going to spend the last few days of John's leave at his home. After a long, cold and dreary journey, we arrived at Birmingham. It was very dark and quite late. Our journey had taken the whole day. From here, John had hoped to get a taxi to take us home. It was a vain hope, for though there were taxis available, no driver would take us beyond the City boundary, even when offered double fare. It was against the law, they said. Possibly due to severe petrol rationing, the City boundary was their limit. Reluctantly we had to agree. There was no alternative. Eventually we were deposited at some cross roads, about four or five miles from our destination. Clutching our luggage, we set out through the intense darkness. When we had been walking for about ten minutes, I suddenly said "John, we are going the wrong way." We were still walking on pavement when we should have been on a country road. The cross roads, in the darkness, had confused us.

We retraced our steps, and started in the right direction, consoling each other by saying how lucky we were that it was neither snowing nor raining. We trudged along for the most part in silence, pausing every now and again to set down our luggage, which seemed to gain weight with each mile.

Very weary and jaded, we at last reached home. The house was in darkness, and the door was locked. Fortunately Punch the Collie, heard our approach and barked a warning. We thought this would surely rouse the household, but not so. Punch soon realised that we were not intruders, and the barking ceased. Once again all was quiet. John picked up a handful of pebbles, which he proceeded to throw at Stafford's bedroom window. At this unusual sound, Punch once again started to bark. Fortunately, this time, the noise wakened Stafford, who soon let us in.

Too tired to sleep, I thought that, at least as far as I was concerned, 'honeymoon' was a definite misnomer.

For private cars, petrol was very severely rationed, and joy riding was strictly prohibited. Cars were only allowed to be used for business purposes, and only then if the question 'Is your journey really necessary" had been answered in the affirmative. Many an unsuspecting calf, or piglet, was bundled into a farmer's car, to camouflage a journey that did not comply with these conditions. Shortage of petrol, and the uncertainty as to our time of arrival had made it impossible for us to be met on our return from Eastbourne.

However, when the day came on which John had to return to France, his father said that Stafford could drive us to Coventry station. John had found that by joining the train there, instead of at Birmingham, he could delay his departure by several hours. So to Coventry Stafford drove us, that cold December morning to catch the train, which left at 3 a.m. I was going to London with John to see him off. Then, as the Christmas holiday was due, I should continue the journey to my home.

When the train drew in, it seemed that every carriage was full. We entered one, in which there were eight soldiers, and we squeezed into a seat. It was literally a squeeze, for the bulky uniforms of the men took up more than the usual room. One soldier very kindly moved to the opposite side, so that John and I could sit together. The men had evidently been asleep, and only some of them had roused as we entered the carriage. Blinds were drawn, only a small dim blue light relieved the darkness. The modicum of fresh air, which had entered with us, was soon dissipated in the thick fug which enveloped the compartment. It was compounded of tobacco smoke and various odours. I dare not suggest opening a window, lest it aroused the sleepers. Who knew? This might be their last chance of a comfortable sleep for a long time.

The soldier on my left had soon settled himself, and as he nodded off to sleep, his head came to rest on my left shoulder. John soon succumbed to the drowsy atmosphere, his head found a resting place on my right shoulder. From the figure on his right came an intermittant snore. As I watched the trails of moisture which trickled down the mirror on the opposite side of the carriage, I became aware of the fact that all eyes were not closed. From the seat facing me, one eye was apparently staring straight at me. At first, I found this most disconcerting, and wondered what it could be that so rivetted its attention. Then I realized that the eye was sightless, not a human eye at all, but an artificial one. Fixed upon me all the time, it added a macabre touch to the strange journey.

When we arrived in London, we found that there had been a Zeppelin raid during the night. The steps to the Underground Railway were blocked with people who had sought shelter there. I followed closely behind John, as he elbowed his way through the teeming crowd. When we reached the departure platform at Victoria, we found it thronged with khaki clad figures, youngsters going for the first time into the holocaust of war, and veterans returning from leave.

At the thought of what lay ahead for some of them, I was so distressed, that I could hardly restrain my tears. My determination to "keep a stiff upper lip" would, I knew, soon crumble. I dare not wait to see the train depart, so, with a last embrace, I stumbled away with misty eyes.

For days after reaching home, I was in a state of stupor. So much had happened in so short a time, so many new sensations and experiences, so many journeys, so little rest, that I was in a daze. It was fortunate that it was holiday time, and I was not called upon to exert myself.

Before returning to school my equanimity was practically restored. Once there, I knew that the demands of my work would leave me no time to brood. In review, the past weeks had already taken on the quality of a dream—or was it a nightmare?

# 17. Spanish Flu

NOT LONG AFTER my return, I realized that a new relationship had developed between Dash and Hugh. Since his brother's death Hugh's visits had been infrequent, but now, he again became a regular visitor. The reason was quite apparent. He made sundry little gifts to Dash, and his visits were invariably on evenings when I was absent at an Operatic rehearsal, or an organ lesson, and she had an evening free from commitments.

To my surprise, Dash seemed to welcome his attentions. I was glad, for she had been particularly reserved since the Howard episode. Never very confiding, she had retreated further than ever into her shell of reticence, so I was unable to gauge her feelings. Perhaps she was at last recovering from the shock she had sustained. She was a pretty girl, with large brown eyes and fair curly hair. More than one young man had sought her acquaintance, only to be shown, in no uncertain manner, that his attentions were unwelcome.

No wonder I was surprised at this new development, for a more dissimilar pair it would be hard to find. Dash was short in build, and often in temper, energetic, fond of dancing, and an excellent tennis player. She seemed full of health and vitality. Hugh, on the other hand, was tall and thin. Because of his poor health, he was unable to take part in any out door sport, and his hobbies were stamp collecting, music, and other sedentary pastimes.

Fortunately, he had a great sense of fun, and was a welcome guest at parties, for he could not only entertain with his music, but knew many parlour games and tricks, and could tell a funny story well. It was no doubt these attributes which appealed to Dash.

Before the winter was over, a severe epidemic spread through the country, and on the Continent as well. It was known as 'Spanish Flu': at first no one realized what a virulent plague this would prove. Dash was one of the first victims. I was wakened one night by her screaming, and muttering. I thought at first that she was having a nightmare. This was not unusual, but when the ramblings continued, I put on the light. At the sight of her face, I knew she was really ill, and this quite alarmed me. Thrusting my feet into slippers, and struggling into my dressing gown, I snatched up my purse. There was a 'phone box at the end of the street, from which I would call a doctor. As I went through the hall, I took a coat from the pegs, and threw it round my shoulders, like a cape. In my slippered feet, I reached the 'phone, and contacted the doctor, who promised to come at once.

When I got back to the house, I found that Mrs Towner had roused. She looked at Dash, and agreed with me that her condition was serious. The doctor soon came. Later on, we realized how fortunate we had been in getting help so soon. As the cases multiplied, this became impossible. The death rate among soldiers and civilians increased to a most alarming extent. Nurses and hospital beds became unobtainable and the usual prescription given was aspirin, and whisky. As the latter was in short supply, it could only be obtained by producing a doctor's certificate.

Fortunately Dash recovered, but she was still very weak, when Mr and Mrs Towner both fell victims to the insidious disease. Mabel escaped the infection, and managed to look after the invalids, and I helped when I was not at school.

Some of the schools had to close because of the shortage of staff and pupils. We managed to keep open, with a skeleton staff. In my classroom, I had an open fire and a kettle. Whenever possible I made hot drinks for the staff that remained. This may have been a help, for no other member succumbed to the dreaded complaint.

Dash was almost well again, and the number of new cases were at last beginning to decline, when I had an S.O.S. from John's home. His Father was very ill with pneumonia, and the rest of the household, including the domestic help, had all taken to their beds with the well known symptoms of the 'Spanish Flu.' Gladys, the younger sister, was the only one who had not fallen a victim, and she was finding it impossible to cope single-handed. No nurse or other help could be obtained, and even Mrs Bates, the waggoner's wife, who could usually be depended on in an emergency, was herself ill in bed.

Gladys begged me, if it was at all possible, to go to her assistance. Had the request been made any earlier, I could not have considered it. With the extra duties at school, and at the 'digs', every moment of my time had been filled to capacity. However, things were improving. Dash was thinking of returning to school. Mr and Mrs Towner were convalescent, and several members of the school staff had returned. I wondered what to do.

Could I get leave of absence? It had never occurred to me to think of such a thing, except on the occasion of my marriage. I took the letter from Gladys to show to the Headmaster, and asked for his advice. He was sympathetic, but said that he could not give me permission. I should have to apply to the Chairman of the Education Committee. This I did, and was granted an interview. I proffered my request. At first I thought it was going to be refused, but when all the circumstances were explained—the number of invalids, the lack of help, and the remote situation—the Chairman relented. He agreed to give me leave, pointing out that my salary would cease, for as long as I was absent.

When I arrived, I thought Gladys looked tired, as if she too, should be in bed. I wondered how she had managed to cope alone, but she said that Mrs Bates and Stafford too, had helped until they became ill, and it was then that she had thought of sending for me. I visited the patients on the first floor, but to reach the maid, a further flight of steps had to be climbed.

Mr Breeden was extremely ill. The doctor, in spite of his many patients, came each day, and we followed his instructions implicitly. Gladys and I decided that we would take alternative night duty, so that one of us could rest and sleep, while the other one sat up. This proved impossible for, by the end of the day we were both utterly exhausted. The house was big, and it was a long way from the bedrooms to the kitchen. Up and down the stairs we went, carrying trays and toilet necessities. We used the main staircase, although it meant traversing the long hall. It would have been unwise to use the shallow steps which led straight into the kitchen, burdened as we were. Modern conveniences had not yet been installed. Lamps had to be filled, wicks trimmed, globes polished each day. Coal for the big kitchen range and the bedroom fires had to be carried from the coal house across the courtyard. Soft water to fill the boiler by the side of the range was carried in buckets from the wash house, which was also across the yard. There was no water laid on upstairs and the only 'convenience' was discreetly concealed in the shrubbery a few yards from the house.

In spite of this fatiguing work Gladys and I managed to keep the insidious germs at bay. As a precaution we dosed ourselves with cinnamon and quinine tablets. Gladys declared that everything we ate tasted of disinfectant which was copiously used. The doctors visits were chiefly on account of Mr and Mrs Breeden, who did not improve as quickly as the younger members. However, when Nell and one of the boys were again on their feet and Mrs Bates had returned to her duties, I felt it was time for me to go back to school. Someone there was doing my work, the staff that had remained fit had already been sadly overworked, the returned invalids would still be far from well, so my duty lay there.

When I met Dash on my return she had some exciting news for me. She proudly displayed her engagement ring with its solitaire. diamond as she told me that Hugh and she were now engaged. We had a little celebration in the 'digs', drinking sherry and eating sponge cakes which Mrs Towner had made with eggs which I had brought back from the farm, and sugar which had been saved during my absence. As I congratulated Dash and Hugh, my fervent wish was that things would turn out happily for them both. Dash would at least be spared the worry, anxiety and fear entailed by marrying a soldier.

On my return to school I found that my place had been taken by another female newcomer, and I had 'gone up' with the boys who had already been in my class for a year. During this time I had got to know them very well, and had become greatly attached to some of them. We enjoyed together the funny situations which occasionally occurred. They were still particularly fond of their singing lessons, and when the few classical songs given in the new syllabus had been learnt, I introduced them to some of the sea shanties and rollicking choruses from the "Scottish Students Song Book." They sang these with gusto, and even the 'growlers' did their best.

It was good to see the children happy, for they were deprived of many of the delights of a normal peace time childhood. Food was limited, they had no biscuits, sweets or chocolate. The supply of these was almost non existent. I often wondered what the boys bought with their Saturday pennies. Money was not scarce in some of the households, for many of the mothers had gone to work in the munition factories. In some of these an explosive was manufactured which affected the skin of the workers, turning it bright yellow. Often as I cycled through the town, I would pass groups of these 'canaries' as they were called. It was said that when one of these 'canaries' gave birth, her baby, too, was yellow. As compensation for this discolouration, the women were paid very high wages.

The war dragged on, but, at last, the tension seemed to be lessening. News was brighter, victories were frequent, and the appalling casualty lists smaller. We had renewed hope that the horror of the last four years might soon be ended.

We could hardly believe the good news when it did come. On this unforgettable morning, lessons were proceeding in the usual way, when suddenly guns boomed, the Church bells, unheard for years, pealed out the glad news. From the street came a great clamour, there was shouting, cheering and singing. For a moment one felt stunned.

The Headmaster, shaken out of his usual sedate and dignified manner, rushed into the classroom, said breathlessly "I want all the boys in the play ground", and then rushed away again.

The boys were affected by the excitement, instead of an orderly march to the playground, our journey there was a mad scramble. To my surprise, several of the boys were waving small Union Jacks, which they had evidently secreted in readiness.

When all the school was assembled, the Head stood on the steps and gave the good news. The boys cheered, as only boys can. Many more flags were waved, and then the National Anthem was sung. I looked at the Headmaster who was beating time. Something was odd, I realized that he was beating in four four time, and quite unaware of it. He was evidently as bemused as I. After more cheers, the school was dismissed, and given a holiday for the afternoon.

Celebration events were rapidly organized all over the town. Dash and I were invited to a hastily improvised dance. For the occasion, I put on my special taffeta frock, and we went, expecting to have an enjoyable evening. We had not been there long when suddenly I was overwhelmed with melancholy. The gaiety seemed forced, dancing was the last thing I felt inclined to do. Into my mind came the memory of the lads we had known, who would never return. Without telling Dash, I slipped away, with my eyes brimming with tears.

I needed to be alone to control my emotion, and to steady the confused thoughts which filled my mind. The feeling of gratitude that the war was over, was mixed with sympathy for the bereaved. There would be no triumphant return for their loved ones. I thought of the maimed, and the blinded, who would never again live a full life, and I offered up a fervent prayer that in the future, sanity would prevail, so that the war, that was now ended, would really prove to be a "war to end wars."

Somehow one had imagined that once hostilities had ceased, the soldiers would be quickly disbanded. This was not so. Demobilization took a long time  and weeks and months went by without any suggestion of John's home coming.

Dash and Hugh had bought a house, and were looking forward to their marriage. Naturally, they spent as much time as possible together, and Dash and I saw less of each other. For the week-end, I often cycled over to Dunton. It was on one of these visits that Mrs Breeden asked me if I would consider coming there to live. John, she said, would soon be home, and it would be ridiculous for me to be in Coventry, and John at Dunton.

At first, I would not entertain the idea. Then, I realized that with Dash's impending marriage, I should be alone in the 'digs', but, on the other hand, I had always been warned against living with 'in-laws'. Still, it did seem stupid for John and me to be apart, when we could be together. For nearly three years—years which 'the locusts had eaten' we had only spent a few brief weeks together. The happy time of courtship, which Dash was now enjoying, had been denied us.

When John wrote, his letter was full of enthusiasm for his Mother's suggestion. He seemed to take it for granted that I should be living at Dunton when he was demobbed. I could not imagine living there with no specific job. I told Mrs Breeden that I would go, but only if a vacancy for a teacher occurred in a school in one of the neighbouring villages so that it was possible for me to continue teaching. Mrs Breeden did not welcome this idea. Soon she hoped, a suitable farm would be found for John, and then he would need his wife with him.

Farms I knew, were not easy to find, especially for rent. The choice, too, was even more limited, because John's father wanted one that was reasonably near his own. Then John would be able to borrow some of the expensive farm machinery. To set up a son in farming needed considerable capital. John, I knew, had scarcely any money of his own. Before joining the army he had received very little in wages from his father. I knew that our expenses would be heavy, and furnishing would be a problem. So, I stuck to my decision. I would only go to Dunton if I could continue teaching.

Surprisingly, a vacancy did occur quite soon, in the nearby village of Minworth. It was three miles from Dunton in the direction of Birmingham. Industry was beginning to spread its tentacles over the district, which was losing its rural character. I put in an application, and was asked to go for an interview. This was held in most opulent surroundings, in what I took to be the Board Room of some local works, in which the Chairman of the school managers had an important position. The meeting was conducted in a most business like way. My testimonials had been read. A few pertinent questions were asked, and then the Chairman said "If you are appointed, will you promise to stay for at least twelve months." I gave this promise and the interview was over. What a contrast it had been to the one at Tadley! I was reminded of the long drive, the homely, rural surroundings, and the farewell gift of daffodils on that occasion.

In a few days, I heard that I had been appointed, and rather sadly, I gave in my month's notice at the school where the work had proved most satisfying to me, with an agreeable staff and a Headmaster who, although he made great demands, was appreciative and just.

When I married, I received from the school a wedding gift of silver spoons and forks. This was the only time that any presentation was made, never when any of the staff left.

The boys that I had taught for so long had recently gone into another class, I was surprised, and most touched, when, on the day I was leaving, their new teacher brought me a present from my old boys. It was a purse of crocodile leather, and inside was a crooked silver threepenny bit for luck. The boys had suggested the gift themselves, the teacher said, and every boy had contributed something. This, I knew, must have meant real self denial for some of them. As it was against school rules, everything had been kept 'sub-rosa'. Stupidly emotional, I had to brush away a tear, as I thanked the boys, and promised to treasure the purse as long as it lasted, and to save the coin to the end of my days.

My 'Goodbyes' were said, and I was alone in the cloak room putting on my hat and coat when, to my surprise, the Head came in. He put his arms round me, gave me a passionate kiss, and saying 'Forgive me, I've wanted to do that for a long time' he hurried from the room. So it was with mixed feelings, and with flushed cheeks that I finally left.

# 18. A VC arrives

THE NEW SCHOOL was very different from the one I had left. Many of the duties which should have been performed by the Head were relegated to the staff. It was usual in a small school for the Head teacher to be responsible for the top class. I was surprised when this was the one allocated to me. As it was a mixed school, I now had to teach adolescent girls as well as boys. The first few days with a new class were always difficult. It was a time when the teacher took the measure of the scholars, and they, in turn, tried out the teacher. Discipline throughout the school was not good, and the children had little respect for the Headmaster.

When once I had learnt their names, things became easier, but it was up hill work, and my patience was often taxed to the utmost, before a satisfactory relationship was established. One boy, Tom Dabbs, was a continual nuisance. His work was poor and untidy, and his intelligence low, but no one could flip a soggy ball of blotting paper so surreptitiously, and with such unerring aim as Dabbs. When questioned, his answers always evoked much merriment from the class, and he was always the centre of noise and mischief. I soon found that caning was no deterrent. He had been accustomed to it throughout his school life.

Many of the children came from a distance to school, as I did, and brought sandwiches to eat at mid-day. Most of the journeys were made on foot, but a few children rode bicycles. Not yet were they conveyed in buses, and given hot meals. When the weather was fine, the two hour break was spent in the playground. As I was the only teacher who stayed, I was supposed to keep an eye on things generally.

One day, when I had finished my sandwiches, I wheeled my bicycle into the playground to clean it. There had been rain in the night, and the roads were very muddy as I cycled to school. I propped the bicycle against a wall where Tom Dabbs was standing. He came and stood near me, his hands in his trouser pockets and his feet apart. I thought it quite possible that he would make some impertinent remark, but he remained silent.

"Do you ride, Tom" I said.

"Yes" he replied scornfully.

He rubbed a finger along the mud guard, and looked at it with derision.

"Do you think you could find me something to scrape away the mud" I said.

He looked at me a little doubtfully, but went off, and shortly returned with a small piece of wood. To my surprise, he bent down and proceeded to scrape away the mud, which had collected in the mud guards. "Gimme a cloth" he said.

Carefully he wiped the strands of the dress guard and each separate spoke of the wheels. Between us, the task was soon finished. "You have made a very good job of your part of it, Tom". Saying this, I handed him a threepenny bit. He gave one of his puckish grins, and looked so pleased, that I said "How would you like to clean the bicycle every week, Tom, for sixpence?" There was no hesitation. "Oh yes please, miss" he replied, and clean it he did, with varying degrees of care, each week.

His behaviour in class started to improve, and the disturbances he caused became less frequent. Was it bribery? or had I merely directed some of his mis-spent energy into more useful channels. I was not sure, but I felt that the end had justified the means.

Each day I missed more and more, the companionship of Dash. There was no one with whom I could discuss the vagaries of school life. At Dunton they seemed completely absorbed in the work and business of the farm. This, naturally, proved of great interest to m e, but I was not permitted to take an active part in any of the farm ac tivi-ties. When I suggested that I might help with the milking, this was treated as a joke, although I assured them that I was quite competent. The garden proved a consolation. There, I could always find some-thing to do, either weeding among the flowers, or hoeing in the kit-chen garden.

The work in the house was well organised, with Mrs Breeden, her daughters Gladys and Nell, Mrs Bates and the maid, there was adequate help. To my great delight, I was asked to gather and arrange the flowers in the various rooms, and so felt that I was helping in a small way.

The girls and their Mother were excellent cooks, and much of their time was taken up in the preparation of food. Each week delicious crusty loaves were baked, and creamy butter churned. Few cakes could be made at this time, because of the shortage of sugar. Each member of the family now drank sugarless tea, or coffee, but the saving here was used to sweeten the puddings, which were made each day. A very old custom was observed at Dunton. The pudding or other sweet was eaten before the meat course. Tarts and fruit pies figured frequently on the menu. The pastry was made from home rendered lard, which was plentiful after a pig had been killed, and the fruit and jam came from the rows of bottles and jars, which filled the store cupboard.

Killing a pig and 'getting it away' was quite a major operation. The first time I witnessed this bizarre ceremony, my feelings were a mixture of fascination and revulsion. First the copper in the washhouse was filled and the fire lit, to ensure plenty of boiling water. Then, on to the yard was dragged from the dairy, a strong wooden bench, Bundles of straw from the rick yard were placed ready. The butcher arrived, accompanied by several children from the village. From its sty, the pig was driven on to the yard, but not without difficulty. Intelligent creature, it sensed that something unpleasant was in store. The pig twisted and turned, and ran in every direction but the one required. Finally, with the children's help, it was headed into the yard, and the door was shut.

I fled into a far room and covered my ears, dreading to hear squeals of pain as the butcher performed his grim task. My fears were groundless I was told, for a humane killer had superceded the knife, and death was instantaneous.

Led by curiosity, I once more watched from the kitchen window. The straw had been ignited, and on this blazing pyre, the pig was laid, like some pagan sacrifice. The children watched with fascination, this temporary incarceration. When the bristles had been scorched off, the carcase was removed from the fire, and placed on the bench. At this point I left the gruesome scene, and turned back into the kitchen.

Gladys had placed ready some wide enamelled pans, which she said were ready for the lard. As soon as the butcher brought in the 'leaf' from the pig, this would be put in the large iron pot on the range to melt, and the resulting lard would be poured into the pans to set. This was all new to me, and I was eager to learn, for I knew that, as a farmer's wife, I should one day have to 'get away' a pig of our own.

Fortunately, the next day was a Saturday, and I was able to watch as the sisters and my mother-in-law dealt with all the cooking necessary to make full use of the pig meat. Quantities of meat had been placed in large dishes on the kitchen table. The sides of the pig, the hams, and the head had been made ready for curing. These would be placed in salt and saltpetre in the large lined trough in the dairy. Some meat was chopped ready for the raised pork pies, some was finely minced, and made into sausages. At this Mrs Breeden was quite adept. When they were made, she twisted the sausages into groups of about six, in a most professional manner. I asked if I might try, but my efforts were not successful. From the liver, and some of the other organs, savoury faggots were made. The meat was mixed with herbs and rolled into balls, which were wrapped in a thin skin which had little pockets of fat in it. This basted the faggots as they cooked.

The smell of the boiling lard from the previous evening still lingered in the kitchen. To this, was added the scent of herbs, the smell of fresh meat, and that of the 'trotters' which were simmering on the hob.

I was most interested in the making of the pork pies. The flour was mixed with hot fat, and the paste was then moulded over the base of some round two-pound jam jars. These were placed on the window sill until the pastry was cool. The resulting shape was filled with the chopped meat, and a decorated pastry lid was put on top. Through a hole in this lid, the glutenous liquor from the 'trotters' was poured. This made the savoury jelly which surrounded the meat in the pies. When all the meat had been dealt with, there remained some bones. They were mostly small, and flat, and had quite a lot of flesh on them. These were placed in a pie dish, and covered with some of the pork pie paste. To eat this delicacy was to discover that 'The nearer the bone, the sweeter the meat', was indeed true.

What a feast the poor pig had provided. Besides the main dishes, there were smaller succulent items, brains on toast, and 'scratchings' the nutty, crisp little nuggets of fat, left behind from the lard. There were also 'chitterlings' but realizing what these were, and having once watched their preparation, I felt that they were better discarded. How true it was, what the country folk claimed, that the only thing about a pig that could not be used, was its squeal.

I now looked forward specially to the school holidays, when I joyfully packed my bag and left for home. It was good to return once again to the long walks and intimate talks with Winifred. I had worried about the state of Mother's health. Letters had warned me that she was far from well, as she was suffering from Angina, and I had been impatient to see her.

Annie had been home recently. She looked quite different, Mother told me, for her beautiful long fair hair had been cut short, and trimmed into the fashionable 'shingle.' Annie had suggested, that now Mother spent so much time in bed, she might find it more comfortable, if she, too, had her hair cut short. Mother had said she would think about it, and she asked for my advice.

I knew that Mother was not averse to change. She had always welcomed any innovation that she thought was beneficial. Mother had presented Father with pyjamas, when most men were still wearing night shirts. The family had thought pyjamas most comical and Harry had put the first pair on, stuffed them out with a cushion, put a paper hat on his head, and played the clown, to everyone's amusement.

Now, I could see that Mother was hesitant about having her hair cut. Personally, I could not imagine Mother with any other hair style than the one she had worn for so long. Her fine, silvery hair was dressed with a roll over the front of her head, and a plaited bun at the back. My own hair was still long and plaited into two coils, one above each ear.

I told her that with any other hair style she would not look like my own dear familiar Mother, so would she please keep it just as it was. Mother gave a look of relief and pleasure, I knew that my advice had been what she secretly hoped for.

No holiday was ever long enough to do all that I had planned. How curiously elastic time can seem. Moments of ordeal seem like hours, and hours of ecstasy fly with incredible speed.

Soon I was once more on my way back to Dunton, and school. As the train hurried me away, I saw my beloved hills gradually recede. The blue of the sky changed to grey, the flowers in the gardnes that we passed, were less brilliant in colour. As we neared the murky, industrial Midlands, I wondered why fate had chosen to uproot me from the home, and environment, to which I was devoted.

When I arrived back at the farm, I found the family in a great state of excitement. Mrs Breeden's sister's son, Cecil, who had been awarded the V.C. was coming to visit them. Cecil was an orphan, both his parents having succumbed to the 'Flu' epidemic. When Cecil was young his family had lived at Lea Marston, a village not far from Dunton. Here, Cecil had attended the village school, before going to the Grammar School in the nearby town of Coleshill.

The news of his visit spread quickly, and in both Lea Marston and Coleshill, it was felt that something should be done to honour this local hero. A committee was formed, and collections were made. It was decided to give Cecil a civic reception, and to present him with an inscribed gold watch. The town band of Coleshill would meet him on his arrival, and he would be escorted in triumph to the Town Hall, for the reception.

The plans were all made, the date, and time of his arrival, were eagerly awaited. Cecil wrote to say that he would arrive on Wednesday afternoon, by a train reaching Water Orton station at two p.m. This news was passed to the Committee, and the last minute arrangements were completed.

Imagine our surprise and dismay when Cecil quietly walked in at Dunton on the preceding Tuesday afternoon. He had managed to get off earlier he told us.

Now we were faced with a problem. How could we arrange for Cecil to be at the station on Wednesday. We could not explain our predicament to him, as we felt that he would not enjoy the prospect of all the fuss that was to be made. He was a big, hefty fellow who, before joining the Army, had spent several years farming in a remote part of Canada.

It was quite impossible to alter the arrangements at such short notice. The people involved were scattered over a wide area, and telephones were few. At first we saw no way out. Then, at last, we hit on a solution. By some means, we must get Cecil back into Birmingham, so that we could arrive back at Water Orton station at the time arranged, on Wednesday.

This, as we expected, was not at all easy. On Wednesday morning, Gladys told Cecil that she and I were going into Birmingham and we would like him to come with us. Cecil said that he did not care much for big towns, so he would much rather look round the farm.

Gladys told him that Wednesday was market day, and Stafford and her Father would be away most of the day. "That's O.K" he said "I'll go with them."

We pretended to be offended, and told him that he would be able to go to many sales, but we did not have many opportunities of going out to lunch with a handsome young man. Father is treating us to our lunch, Gladys went on, and it will be the best that we can find. If you go to the sale, you will only have bread and cheese.

We began to think our efforts were in vain, but at last, he yielded to our persuasions, and reluctantly agreed to accompany us. Our fictitious business was soon finished, and we had lunch. This was not nearly as good as the one we should have eaten at Dunton, but it had served our purpose.

As we seated ourselves in the train back to Water Orton, Gladys and I looked at each other with a smile, and each gave a sigh of relief.

We neared the station, and could hear rousing music from the band. The train slowed down, and the waiting crowd cheered lustily. Wondering what all the noise was about, Cecil looked out of the window. Two uniformed men seized the handle of the carriage door and were about to open it, when Cecil bristled, and looked most pugilistic. Had he a guilty conscience? Was he expecting arrest? We really knew little of his activities.

I caught his arm and said "They have come to welcome you, Cecil. The band is in your honour." He gave me a funny look, straightened his jacket, squared his shoulders, and stepped out. The two men seized him, and he was carried shoulder high from the station. Flags waved, the crowd shouted and cheered, and the band played as Cecil rode, with some of the civic dignitaries in the ceremonial car, to the reception.

Stafford was waiting for us. The car, like several others, was all a flutter with pennants. We made our way slowly through the milling people, some of whom were carrying banners bearing slogans which read 'Welcome to Cecil, our gallant V.C.'

After the reception, when the speeches had been made, and the watch presented, Cecil was driven to visit the Grammar School. Here, there were more speeches, and then Cecil was taken round his native village, and to the small school. All the inhabitants who were able, had congregated in the school playground, which had been decorated for the occasion. Congratulations were given and reminiscences were exchanged among those who had known Cecil before he left the village. Finally, 'he was returned to Dunton.

The local press made much of the occasion, the papers were full of photographs, and details of the proceedings. As I read the graphic account which they gave, I smiled a quiet little smile, as I thought how narrowly Gladys and I had averted a fiasco.

# 19. Heights and Depths

JOHN'S FATHER was still continuing his search for a farm. Particulars were sent to him from various agents but, so far, nothing suitable had appeared. The most promising ones were all too far away; I began to wonder if Mr Breeden would ever be successful in his quest. Whatever happened, I should still have to fulfil my promised year of teaching.

At last, some eagerly anticipated, and long awaited news came. John was being demobilised, and would soon be home.

My hopes ran high. Now, I should once again have a companion, and we could really begin to plan our future. Things did not turn out quite as I anticipated. Naturally enough, John was made much of by the family but not only by the immediate relations. Uncles, Aunts, and cousins, of whom there seemed to be a legion, all had to be visited. It was indeed, a veritable clan into which I had married. Members had remained, married, and died, in the vicinity, for generations. In the neighbouring churchyards, many of the oldest tombstones bore their names. As we paid visit after visit, I wondered if I should ever remember all the varying degrees of relationship. Almost all of them were farming or in occupations connected with the land.

Much of the leisure, which I had hoped to spend with John, was taken up by these visits. We had scarcely finished the round, before the return visits began. It seemed a very closely knit community. All were very hospitable, and visits usually meant a gargantuan meal, followed by an evening of card playing. For me, cards had been an occasional relaxation, but now it seemed to be part of the pattern of every day life. As soon as the meal was over, in the long dark evenings, the cards were produced. Sometimes we would have a game in which all could join, or a mild gamble with penny 'nap.' Mother-in-law still had a passion for Bridge, and John and I were usually called upon to make up the necessary four.

Although I was fond of Bridge, there were many evenings when I would have preferred other occupations. The only time I had for writing letters, or the preparation of my school work, was at the week-end. During the week, John and I were both busy. While I was at school, he was helping on the farm. On Saturday afternoons, John and Stafford would often go into Birmingham to watch their favourite football team. Sometimes, as an alternative, they would go out with their guns, and return with a mixed bag of perhaps pheasant, partridge, hare and rabbit.

This was the time that I should have liked to spend with John, but I knew how greatly he enjoyed both football and shooting. He had gone without these pleasures for so long, that I felt it would be unfair to suggest that he should forego them, to spend the time with me. Sunday afternoons were practically the only time we had together, free from the demands of the family.

John had not been home very long, before I had a suspicion that I might be pregnant. To have a family was my dearest wish, but I had not anticipated starting one before we were in a home of our own. Until my suspicions were confirmed, I decided to say nothing, even to John. Somehow, I did not think his Mother would welcome the news, especially if we were still at Dunton when the baby arrived. Even when I was sure, I kept the secret to myself; although it was difficult to keep the tell-tale symptoms from the family.

One Saturday afternoon when John and Stafford had gone to a football match, my mother-in-law asked me if I would go with Nell and herself, to visit a neighbouring farm. This was the home of the Pridhams, a childless couple who doted on horses. On one of their frequent visits to Dunton, Mr Pridham had asked me if I could ride. I told him that I could not, but that I would dearly like to learn. Whereupon he offered to teach me.

When we arrived at the farm, the maid told us that the Pridhams were in the far meadow. We stabled the pony, and set out to find them. When greetings had been exchanged, Mr Pridham said "Now, young lady, what about a ride,"
"Oh no!" I said, "Not today."

"Never a better time" he replied, and without more ado, he hoisted me on to the horse, by which he was standing. As soon as we started round the field, I had a feeling of nausea.
"Please take me off" I begged, but Mr Pridham only laughed, and accelerated the pace of the horse. Again, I asked to be put down, but my distress was treated as a joke, and I knew that without making a great fuss, I should have to endure the discomfort, till the joke palled.

When he finally lifted me down, my pallor was commented upon, but it was put down to fright, and no further notice was taken.

During the following week, I felt far from well. I had a persistent headache, something to which I was unaccustomed. The three mile cycle ride to school, was a toil. Perhaps it was my imagination, but the wind seemed to be always against me, and to blow with extra vigour, so as to impeded my progress. On the Saturday, John went to Birmingham, to have a suit fitted, and I went with him.

John had found on his return home, that his wardrobe was sadly depleted. He and Stafford wore the same size in clothes. No material, however durable, could resist for long, the wear and tear of the heavy farm work. While John had been away 'coupons' had been introduced, so instead of buying new clothes for himself, Stafford had worn those left behind by John. Coupons were still required, so each member of the family had contributed some, so that John's wardrobe could be replenished.

The tailor's workroom, where John was fitted, was at the top of a long flight of stairs. In each shop that we visited, we seemed to be confronted by more and more stairs. Never before, had I noticed their multiplicity. With each flight that we ascended, I felt more unwell. Never had I been more thankful to reach home. I lay prone upon the bed for a while with head and back both throbbing with pain. Stupidly, I told no one of my discomfort. Ignorant as I was I wondered if I was merely suffering the usual concomitants of pregnancy: if so, as this subject was taboo, I must suffer in silence.

On Sunday, by pleading excess of school work, I was able to spend a quiet day, but that night I could not sleep. Wave after wave of pain enveloped me. John slept peacefully, but when I gave an involuntary cry, he roused. Drowsily he said "What's wrong?" I gave an evasive answer, and he again slept. Why I behaved in this foolish stoical manner, I shall never know. Surely this, of all times, was when I needed symapthy, and some of the cherishing we had promised in our marriage vows. All this would have been forthcoming, if only I had told John how I was suffering.

At last, with one overwhelming pain, I gave a loud cry, and knew that now, there would be no baby. John sat up in alarm. "Whatever is the matter" he said. A moan was his only answer, and he rushed to fetch his mother. Rather ungraciously, she did what was necessary, and saying "You will be alright now", she went back to bed.

In the morning, I still felt very ill. I knew that this was the day on which John and his Father were to attend a local farm Sale, in the hope of purchasing some cattle. Before he went, I asked John if he would send for the doctor. He promised that he would do so before going to the Sale. The doctor arrived. After examining me, he said that a slight operation was necessary, and it was urgent. He would go at once to fetch the operating surgeon.

When he had gone, I asked for a pencil and paper, and drafted out my will. If I died, which, feeling as I did, I thought was a possibility, I wanted my few treasures to be shared between Winifred and Dash. I knew it was not a legal document, but I hoped that my wishes would be honoured.

This effort exhausted me. I lay inert until the surgeon arrived. The operation was completed. I had returned to consciousness, before John and his Father returned from the Sale. John, of course, was very concerned, and said that if he had known what was to happen, he would never have left me.

For my convalescence, I was moved into the guest room. Never before had I realized how noisy the farm house was. Being on a hill, there always seemed to be a breeze, doors were continually banging. Milk buckets clanked loudly, the crow of the cockerells seemed extra shrill. Even the cows seemed to moo more frequently, and one, whose calf had been taken from her, complained raucously all day long. There was no peace for my jangled nerves.

As I lay, I thought how unutterably stupid I had been in concealing my pregnancy, especially from John. But, if he alone had known, the unfortunate horse ride, which was responsible for the trouble, would still have occurred. It was no use brooding. I must concentrate on getting well, and returning to school. The household was a busy one, and an invalid did not fit at all well into the scheme of things. I soon began to feel that I was somewhat of a nuisance, I knew from my own experience, what a trial it was to carry trays, and other impedimenta, on the long trail from the kitchen.

Disinclined to read, and unable to sleep during the day, I occupied myself by trying to decipher the complicated pattern of the material which draped the large half tester bed, in which I lay.

Then, with the thought of School of Art in mind, I tried to discover the unit of design in the exotic wallpaper. Flamboyant flowers grew at the base of leafy palm trees, on the branches of which, gaily coloured parrots perched. There was plenty to interest me in this way, for curtains, and upholstery, all were patterned.

When I returned to school, the wind seemed to blow against me with greater frequency, and, strange though it seemed, the way appeared to be uphill both going and returning. Fortunately, the Christmas holiday was near. In a few weeks I should be able to visit home once more. When I told John that I wanted to go home for Christmas, he begged me to stay at Dunton. He particularly wanted to spend this Christmas, the first since the war, with his parents. I could quite understand how he felt, but at the same time I realized that my own Mother would not be spared to us for many more years. In fact, this might be her last Christmas as her state of health was so precarious.

Reluctantly, we decided to spend Christmas apart. As soon as the vacation started, I set out for home. The day was fine and dry.
As the train passed through the suburbs of Birmingham, I had a bird's eye view of the dreary terraced houses, which fringed the City. In some of the small gardens varicoloured clothes, which had been hung to dry, drooped with never a flutter. Here and there, a garden showed signs of care, but most of them seemed to be frilled with a heterogeneous assortment of rubbish.

The train gathered speed, and as the scene became more rural, the day brightened, the sky was tinged with blue. John had come with me to the station, and had bought me a newspaper, and a magazine. These lay unread upon my lap, as I watched the changing scene, and thought with pleasurable anticipation of my forthcoming visit.

Stanley was to be at home with Margaret, his wife. Stanley, too, had married during the war. Most of his training had been in Ireland and, while there, he had fallen in love. Before leaving he had married Margaret. Unfortunately, no member of Stanley's family was able to be present, but we had all received a glowing account of the ceremony, and many photographs. Stanley was now teaching in a London grammar school, and he and Margaret had spent several week-ends at home. Mother, in her letters to me, had written very fondly of Margaret, and I was all agog to meet my new sister-in-law.

Margaret had very blue eyes, and a mass of black curly hair. She looked a picture of health, and was energetic and capable. At the same time she was most affectionate, and her manner to Mother was kind and sympathetic. When Margaret heard me telling Mother of my mishap, she was most concerned, and, in spite of my protests, insisted on bringing my breakfast to bed each morning. Although I was usually an early riser, and very independent, I must admit that I enjoyed this cossetting, and my heart warmed towards Margaret. Stanley, I thought, was very lucky to have found such a pretty and aimiable wife.

Our tongues were kept busy with all the items of family news that had to be exchanged. The recent letters from Harry and Annie had been kept for my perusal, and I was brought up to date with their affairs. On most days we had a visit from Winifred and Olive. Their lives seemed to be moving in the same uneventful routine. Winifred was now teaching in Brighton, where she went each day by the familiar train of 'Centre' days. Olive was concentrating on music, of which she intended to become a teacher. Neither of them had a beau. Lewes was mostly a residential town. Quite a large proportion of the population was composed of elderly retired people. There were few industries in the town: most of the young men who had returned from the war, were employed elsewhere. Living a quiet life with a widowed Mother, the two girls had little opportunity of meeting men, eligible or otherwise. I hoped that fate would be kind, so that romance would one day enrich their lives.

The holidays sped by. Rest, cossetting, and the happy Christmas atmosphere had all contributed to my well being. It was with a feeling of renewed health that I journeyed back to Dunton.

Here I was greeted with the good news that Father-in-law had at last found a farm for John. It was in the hamlet of Lea Marston, only two miles from Dunton. From the high ground, on which Dunton stood, the ground gradually sloped away to a river, and it was on the low lying ground near the river that the farm stood. It was called the "Hollies".

I could hardly wait to see it, and was impatient for the next morning to arrive. Unfortunately the day was dull and inclined to drizzle. The flat, low lying water logged fields which surrounded the house looked depressing. The house itself was large  three stories high facing West. I felt vaguely disappointed. In imagination I had pictured our future home as a long low house, veiled with creepers, bathed in perpetual sunshine. This tall stark house looked forbidding with no shrubs or bushes to soften its outline. Rain dripped from the bare branches of the trees which grew in a small spinney opposite the farm house. As we approached the door, a loose brick squelched, spattering me with mud.

I reminded myself of how difficult it had been to find a farm and how fortunate we were that at last we were to have a home of our own. Perhaps when the sun shone things would look more cheerful. We had certainly chosen a depressing day for a first visit.

John was already acquainted with the tenants, an elderly childless couple, who had been at the "Hollies" for a long time and were now about to retire.

I was introduced before being shown over the house. The kitchen with its shiny red tiled floor and the glowing fire was cosy and cheerful, but the rest of the house, with the exception of one bedroom, appeared unused. Most of the paint work was a drab brown in colour. wallpapers were faded and nondescript. The windows were all closely curtained, with roller blinds drawn about one third of the way down. From the fusty smell of the rooms I thought it unlikely that the windows were ever opened.

There were five rooms on the first floor, three of them furnished as bedrooms. One of the others had a concrete floor. This was known as the 'cheese room.' At the top of the house were three large attics empty except for one in which was an old oak four poster bed. The attic walls were festooned with cobwebs which hung like grey gauzy veils from every corner and crevice.

My mind was soon busily engaged in planning the alterations that could be made when John and I moved in.

The tenancy of the farm terminated on the twenty fifth of March. My promised year of teaching finished at the end of February. In these intervening weeks, I attended several farm sales with John. Farms rarely changed hands, but when they did, the move was generally made at the March quarter. Besides cattle and machinery, some surplus furniture was often included in the sales. While John was busy among the cows and pigs, the ploughs and drills, I sought bargains in furniture and kitchen necessities. The amazing number of things required for running a home surprised me. Prices in the shops were very high at this time, and with our limited means it was quite impossible to buy some of the things that we really needed. These farm sales proved a happy hunting ground. There were no catalogues for the furniture, so the desired article had first to be found, the number noted, and a vigilant eye kept upon the auctioneer. The first sale I attended was quite an ordeal. Packed closely with people, the room became very stuffy. The fast rate, at which the bids were taken, was quite bewildering, it was often difficult to make sure which lot was actually being sold. No bargains were secured on this first occasion. All I did acquire, was knowledge of the procedure, and also a racking headache, which fortunately soon disappeared when I was once more in the fresh air.

Other sales proved more rewarding. I obtained china, kitchen utensils, chairs and oddments of furniture, at a fraction of the price asked by the shops.

Valuation, and all the other necessary details which had to be attended to when a farm changed hands, were completed. The tenants left, and the house was now empty. It was on a blustery March day, that we took possession. Fleecy cumulus clouds, like bales of cotton wool, scudded across the sky, as we loaded the float, ready for our departure from Dunton. It was a heterogeneous collection that we piled into the float. There were cleaning materials, chairs, a kettle, some kindling, cups, and a tin of coffee, and on top of all, a feather bed. On this soft seat I sat, as we drove on the downhill road to the "Hollies."

Fortunately, the house had been scrubbed through before being left. In spite of this, the rooms seemed forlorn and dingy. Our voices echoed in the emptiness and the paint and shabby wall coverings seemed even more drab than before.

We soon unpacked the float, and while John kindled a fire in the kitchen range, I filled the kettle. The water in the tap over the sink was from a rain water tank, set on stilts by the side of the house. Drinking water had to be pumped from a well, in the cooling house across the yard.

The kitchen fire was soon burning merrily. John then lit one in the long room adjoining the kitchen. This we intended to use as a dining and sitting room combined. It was a big room and had two doors near together, both opening into the hall. We assumed from this, that at some time, two rooms had been made into one. The fire here burned sluggishly, and soon smoke was billowing into the room from the unswept chimney—another job for immediate attention. Stafford John's brother, had promised to follow us, bringing with him a load of furniture. As we awaited his arrival, we made a tour of inspection outside. John, of course, had seen the buildings, but it was all new to me. Across the near yard, was the cooling house, so called because it housed the apparatus whereby the milk which came warm from the cow, was cooled before being marketed. Here too, was the pump and a large copper.

When we had milk to sell, this copper would have to be filled each day and the fire lit under it, John said, so that the milking utensils could be sterilized in the boiling water.

Near the cooling house was a door through which lay the kitchen garden. This looked sadly neglected and overgrown. I wondered how long it would be before I could create some order out of the chaotic mess.

Behind a jutting wall, we found the privy coyly hidden. Inside this primitive convenience was a long, scrubbed seat containing accommodation for two adults. At the side was a small replica, evidently for a child. Hanging within reach were small squares of newspaper. This communal effort greatly amused us, and we promptly named it the 'three-seater.' Was any family so well regulated, we wondered, that they felt the call of nature at the same moment. If so, did they sally forth hand in hand? We burst into laughter at the very absurdity of the idea.

There were two other buildings in this yard, a large fowl pen, and the stable, both built of brick. On the other side of a dividing wall were the cowsheds and the barn. Beyond these lay the rickyard, surrounded by meadows which ran down to the river.

We had no time for further investigation for Stafford arrived with the furniture, among which was our most expensive purchase so far, a Sheraton style bedroom suite.

After our first visit to the farm, John and I had decided to use for our own, one of the large bedrooms in the front of the house, and it was with this in mind that we had bought the suite. This bedroom, as well as two of the others, and also the long sitting room, had the floors covered with linoleum. We had purchased this from the out-going tenants. Although it was not what we should have chosen, we thought it would be better than bare boards, till we could afford something more to our liking.

The stairs, which led off the side hall, were narrow, and had a sharp bend about half way up. It needed careful manipulation to get even some of the smaller pieces of furniture to the top, and John and

Stafford agreed that to attempt this feat with the mahogany wardrobe would be hopeless. I was very disappointed when it had to be placed in an empty room on the ground floor.

As I worked, I could not help thinking how much nicer every-thing would have looked if the rooms could have been decorated, before we moved in. John had approached the landlord to see if he would consider this, but he had not proved very amenable.

When it began to get dark, we finished for the day. John had bought two hanging lamps, one for the kitchen and one for the sitting room, but these were not ready for use.

Mrs Breeden had suggested that we should sleep at Dunton until our house was in order. This offer we gladly accepted, and there we went, tired and dirty. Very grateful we felt for the hot bath, and good meal, which were provided without any effort on our part.

For several days we took a picnic lunch and worked at the "Hollies" till dusk. While I was busy in the house, John was attending to the farm work, which allowed no respite. The fields, unlike the house and the cow sheds, had not been left empty. After harvest, the fields had been ploughed and resown, the cost of the labour, and the value of the growing crops had been estimated, and paid for, when the farm was taken over. There was still much to be done, besides ploughing and sowing. The cowsheds were whitewashed and dis-infected, ready for their new occupants: for days a bonfire of rubbish was kept burning.

Two of the farm hands previously employed on the farm, had asked if they could work for John, and to this he had agreed. The men were natives of the village, and lived in the farm cottages. One man was elderly, named 'Loll.' the other, whose age was about forty, was known as 'Bodger.' Loll was short and rotund, with a ruddy round face from which sprouted an incipient red beard. Bodger had dark straggly hair. He was tall, thin, and cadaverous looking. His looks certainly dispelled the illusion that all country dwellers were healthy and robust. Both he and Loll had done nothing but farm work since leaving school. Loll was the cowman, and Bodger, the waggoner, but both were able to do any of the jobs on the farm, and much of the work was shared.

The arable fields were separated from the rest of the farm by the main road. They lay on either side of a narrow lane, and the farthest fields were a long way from the house. When the men were away working in these fields, the house was strangely quiet. Not yet was there any cackling of hens, or lowing of cattle.

One afternoon I had my first callers. A neighbouring farmer's wife, Cissie, came with a friend Peggy. While I was showing them over the house, I said how sorry I was that no decorating had been done. Peggy said:-

"Why not do some yourself?"

"I really should not know how to begin" I replied.

"Well" said Peggy, "If you would like to have a go, I will come and help you. I have done quite a lot."

I thanked her warmly, and told her, that though the idea had never occurred to me, I thought it was an excellent one. She told me what materials to get, and promised to come as soon as I was ready to begin.

When John came home and I told him of Peggy's suggestion, he was not at all enthusiastic. He was quite agreeable that we should try, but preferred to reserve his opinion until the job was done. How different his reaction was from mine. Already my ebullient and optimistic imagination had pictured the walls with their new coverings, the paintwork sparkling and fresh. However, John promised to buy what was required, when next he went to market.

To my surprise and delight, Peggy who lived in a suburb of Birmingham, arrived the next morning, with a book of wallpaper patterns. We spent a pleasant time choosing one for the sitting room and a suitable one, for the bedroom. When John was asked for his opinion, he approved our choice.

Peggy then measured the rooms and estimated the amount of paper required. This she promised to order, and to bring as soon as possible.

Paint and paper, distemper and brushes were assembled and the morning arrived when the onslaught was to begin. Peggy and Cissie both arrived quite early, and Cissie brought an extra white-wash brush and bucket. We tied up our hair in dusters, donned our overalls, and began. Cissie had decided that the kitchen should be the first room to receive attention. The strong kitchen table proved to be just the right height for the ceiling to be reached with ease. Soon Peggy and Cissie were both mounted upon the table and slap dashing away with vigour. To begin with, I was allocated the role of observer, but I busied myself by trimimng the rolls of wallpaper ready for the next operation.

What fun we had! Even the few mishaps only provoked laughter. Peggy and Cissie came each day until the allotted task was finished. They brushed aside my thanks, saying that had really enjoyed themselves, and offered to come and help again on some future occasion. I thought how fortunate I was to have found such friends.

The final result of our labours—for I, too, had been allowed to help with the papering—delighted me. I decided that by degrees, each room in the house, should be so transformed.

There was no time for the moment, to continue with this new and rewarding occupation, for the garden needed immediate attention. I hoped that the men would have time to deal with the kitchen garden. but, for the present, they were far too busy.

The weather was fine, and soon I managed to clear and dig a small patch, where I planted some lettuce, radishes, and broad beans. Fortunately, the soil was fairly light, and not the heavy clay which occurred in some of the fields.

Next, I turned my attention to the front garden. Here, there was a lawn, and a long herbaceous border. This was a sorry mess of docks and nettles, mixed with the dried stalks of chrysanthemums and michaelmas daisies. The surface of the bed was almost as grassy as the lawn itself. Everything would have to come out, and the ground be cleared before planting was possible.

I borrowed the farm wheelbarrow, and as I trundled it to and fro with its load of rubbish, I made a mental note that a lighter one must be added to my list of future purchases. The list was already a long one, and again I was amazed at the extraordinary number of things one required in order to furnish adequately a home and garden of one's own.

Soon, the farm began to come alive. John had acquired a spaniel puppy which we named Frisk, an adorable, mischievous, but most companionable little dog. Now in the cowshed were two cows, Blossom and Beauty which John had purchased at the market. Beauty was dry, and would not be milked again until her calf was born. Blossom was an excellent milker, and as we were not yet selling milk, I had a copious supply to deal with, even when the men had received their quota—one of the many 'perks' of a farm labourer.

In the small dairy, which led from the kitchen, was a thrall, a long slate slab supported by brick pillars. On this was placed some wide shallow enamel pans, into which the milk, not needed for immediate consumption, was poured. When the cream rose, it was skimmed from the surface by a perforated metal disk. I had borrowed a small glass churn from Cissie. Into this the cream was poured, the handle turned, and soon the yellow globules of butter appeared in the buttermilk. After being washed, salted, and worked, the butter was then patted into shape.

Making a small quantity in this way, was quite a pleasure. When I thought of the churning day at Dunton, I was glad that all our milk would be sold, and butter making would not be one of my weekly chores.

Many times I had helped by turning the large wooden churn, when the cream proved recalcitrant. Sometimes, it seemed as if the butter would never come. Round and round the churn was turned, a tedious and exasperating job. Then, too, the washing up and scouring afterwards was quite a task. The many parts of the separator—which removed the skim milk from the cream—as well as the churn, butter pats, and every thing used, had to be scalded. If this was not done with meticulous care, the butter was tainted.

# 20. Flood

As soon as the house and garden were in reasonable order, I was
anxious to start poultry keeping. Any money from the sale of
eggs was by custom regarded as 'pin money' for the farmer's
wife. This was not my only incentive. I sometimes wondered if I
were guilty of 'showing off,' and trying to prove to John's Mother
that all teachers were not unsuitable as farmer's wives. Her criticism
still rankled. But I knew that this was not really the motive that
spurred me on. I was genuinely interested in everything to do with
the farm and anxious to take part in anything that was possible.

Cissie, among her many kindnesses, had loaned me a broody hen.
This fowl had finished laying and proved by her continual Cluck!
Cluck! Cluck! that she was eager to sit and produce a family. Near
the large roost on the yard, some small pens had been built into the
wall, specially to accommodate sitting hens. Each had a little wooden
door with a latch. In one of these, I placed a cosy nest containing
thirteen eggs. The door was left open, and some corn put nearby.
Fortunately the hen was a quiet one and when she was put down, she
pecked up a grain or two before she spotted the eggs. Treading
delicately she at once walked in to the pen. She squatted down, and
shuffled her body from side to side, until all the eggs were safely
covered. Then satisfied, she relaxed, content to be immured for the
three weeks necessary before the chickens emerged. Each morning
she would be let out so that she could drink, eat and relieve herself,
before she returned to the nest.

At one of the farm sales I bought, quite cheaply, an incubator which held a hundred eggs. If I could manage this successfully, it would be a quick way of increasing my stock. The natural way with sitting hens would have been less of a risk, but it was difficult to obtain broody hens in any quantity. Enough fertile eggs were bought to fill the tray of the incubator. They were from fowls of various breeds. I did not yet know enough to be discriminating. An oil lamp supplied the heat necessary to hatch the eggs. This was filled, trimmed and lit, the thermometer placed where it could be easily read.

Each morning the tray of eggs was removed from the incubator, so that the eggs could cool. Before replacing the tray each egg was turned over. The sitting hen turned hers with her feet and beak every morning, when she returned to the nest.

I was also able to buy another broody hen, but she was more wild than the placid one from Cissie. The first time I let her off to feed she scuttled away at great speed. Cissie's hen never strayed far from the pen. She had a dust bath, satisfied her other requirements and soon returned to the nest. When there was still no sign of the newcomer I was afraid the eggs would get too cold.

After quite a search, I found her in the farthermost corner of the rickyard, still feeding.

In my ignorance of hens, I tried to drive her towards the pen. She eluded me at every turn. My efforts to catch her were in vain. Feeling foolish and exasperated, I gave up the attempt. Fortunately she returned to her nest. Each day she remained off a long time, but I never again attempted to induce her to return. She eventually had a good hatch, so my anxiety was unnecessary.

As time passed, I reared many chickens, but to me, hens always appeared stupid, motivated by instinct alone, with little, if any, intelligence. Geese and ducks were far more individual, and they afforded me much interest and amusement. For some I felt quite an affection, whereas for some Guinea-fowl which I later acquired, I had a positive dislike. These slate coloured birds, with their white spots, had a flat almost two dimensional look. All day long they uttered their raucous cries which sounded like 'Go back! Go back!' They were spiteful, and often gave the other fowls a vicious peck. Much time I had to spend in hunting for their eggs which they laid in hedge bottoms, or in some other secret and unlikely spot. Fortunately these proved most tasty when eaten, as did the birds themselves.

Soon after we had moved into the farm, John suggested that we should change our bedroom to the one over the kitchen. This overlooked the yards, and was within earshot of the fowl pens, stable and cowsheds. From here, any unusual noise or disturbance would be more readily heard.

As soon as the suggestion was made, I remembered the old oak four poster bed in the attic. The idea of using it did not appeal to John, but he helped to take it to pieces. There was no trace of woodworm. When the posts were polished, they gleamed with the lovely patina which is only acquired by age.

A new mattress had to be specially made, as the bed was wider, and a little shorter than was usual. Being extravagant for once, I bought some beautiful hand block printed material for the cover and curtains of the bed. When all was finished and it was in situ, John was quite impressed, and it was duly admired by Cissie and Ted. They were frequent visitors and it was with Ted's help that the refractory wardrobe had finally reached its position in the front bedroom. When he first made the suggestion that it would have to be sawn in half, I was horrified, but once it was in place no damage was visible.

More cows had been added to Beauty and Blossom. The milk was now being sold to two brothers, Bob and Donald, who had a retail round in one of the Birmingham suburbs. We knew them quite well, as they had bought milk from Dunton for several years.

As the buckets of milk were filled they were carried from the cowshed to the cooling house. Here the milk was tipped into a tank above the cooler, down the corrugated sides of which, the milk slowly found its way into the churns. Into the mouth of the churn was fitted a metal bowl, the base of which was made of fine mesh. Over this was placed a milk wad, a disposable piece of material resembling flannelette. This trapped any cow hairs, that might have fallen into the milk.

Cold water ran through the interior of the cooler. This reduced the temperature of the warm milk, and helped to retain its freshness. When milking was over, and the churns had been rolled away, it was time for me to start the scouring and sterilizing of the things which had been used.

My venture with the incubator proved quite successful and I found it of absorbing interest. When the three weeks were over, I watched with fascination as the eggs began to move jerkily about in the tray. Then there was a faint Peep! Peep! and a star shaped crack appeared in one of the shells. Suddenly a tiny beak was thrust through the shell, and the egg wobbled more vigorously.

It was past our usual bedtime and John had gone to bed some time before, but I was too interested to want to leave. I felt that I must watch this miracle in which I had played a small part. In a short time the chick emerged. It was far from beautiful as it lay damp, dark and apparantly exhausted. Soon other small beaks were beginning to appear.

At this point John gave a peremptory knock on the bedroom floor, and like a good wife I went up to bed. Too excited to sleep, I crept down in the small hours to see how things were progressing. Only a few more chicks had emerged, but what a transformation there was in the morning. The tray was full of yellow downy chicks, pecking and lively, and seeming quite at home in the strange world in which they found themselves.

Encouraged by my success, I thought I would next try to rear some ducks. There were two ponds in the meadow near the house and, in imagination, I already saw them alive with a fluttering, bobbing flock.

I procured a sitting of duck eggs and a broody hen. The pens I had been using were too dry for these I was told, as ducks usually made their nests in a damp situation.

By the side of the house was another small yard in which were three pig sties. Only one was occupied. In this was Chloe, a sow, which John had bought, and which we hoped would soon produce for us a litter of piglets. In the corner of one of the empty sties, I found an ideal site for the nest. Here, the hen would be uninterrupted, have plenty of room for exercise, and could, if she wished, fly over the low wall. She settled down serenely. As I closed the pig sty door, I hoped she would behave well for the whole of the four weeks before the duck eggs hatched.

This month of waiting was nearly up. when Winifred came to stay. This was her first visit to the farm and she was most interested in everything. The district was new to her, too, and she expressed a wish to see Birmingham. A day in the town would be a treat, for I had little opportunity of going there. The buses ran on only two days of the week, leaving at ten o'clock in the morning and returning at six o'clock in the evening. It was a long time to be away from my many duties. We chose a day on which to go and I got up extra early that morning.

The fowls and the chickens were fed, the milk things scoured, the lamps trimmed, the other necessary household chores completed. Into the oven, I put a casserole of meat and vegetables and a milk pudding for John's lunch. Then with a last look at the hen on the duck eggs, which were due to hatch at any moment, we set out for town. Winifred wished to buy a frock, and we spent the morning looking round the various shops till she found what she wanted. The many pretty things we saw were very tempting, but I managed to resist the temptation to buy anything new for myself. There were many things I needed more urgently than clothes.

After lunch, we went to the cinema, and when we had had a cup of tea, we caught the bus for home, having enjoyed the day to the full.

As soon as we arrived, I went to the pig sty, wondering if I should find a nest full of downy ducklings. To my surprise, the wooden gate of the sty was open. I knew quite well that I had shut it as usual. Where the nest should have been was a scrabble of straw, no nest, no hen, no downy ducklings, not even an eggshell. Could they have been moved? I hurried to ask John and from him received some sad news. Chloe the sow, had taken it into her head to emerge from her sty. By some means she had opened the other pig sty door and had made a succulent meal of the contents of the nest. John had seen Chloe wandering in the yard, but the mischief was then done. The hen had evidently flown away in panic.

After my eager anticipation, it was a severe blow. Tears came to my eyes, and I wondered if I could have averted the calamity if I had remained at home. Fortunately, as time passed I grew less sentimental, and learnt to accept more philosophically the various fatalities and mishaps, that occurred among the animals and fowls.

When I did succeed in producing a hatch of ducklings, I had to try not to get too fond of the attractive little creatures. They were most appealing I thought. The small fluffy heads would turn sideways as they looked up at one with their bright eyes, and they certainly possessed more individuality than the chicks. Although I was very fond of roast duck, I resolutely pushed into the background the thought of their ultimate fate.

When my chickens had grown sufficiently for me to determine their sex, I found that more than half of them were cockerells. This was disappointing, as there would be fewer eggs in the future. As time went on however, they provided us with many a tasty meal, and I knew that if I kept them till Christmas, they would find a ready sale.

To my surprise and delight, John arrived back from market one day with two geese. Unlike hens, geese lay their eggs only in Spring. These had evidently finished for the season, and I should have to wait a long time for my first goose eggs. However, I was very pleased to add the handsome white birds to my flock, and I named them Jane and Susan.

I found that there was a prevalent idea among the country folk, that it was a good thing to keep geese with a herd of cows. It was supposed that their presence prevented the spread of a contagious disease, which caused the cows to drop their calves prematurely. It smacked of superstition, and sounded like an old wives' tale to me, but there was often a germ of truth in these old notions, and I wondered if, may be, the droppings from the geese added a tonic quality to the grass.

Some farmers however, looked upon geese as a liability, rather than an asset, for three geese were said to eat as much grass as a cow. As I watched Jane and Susan ceaselessly cropping, I could well believe this.

Time passed and everything was going well. The farm had really come to life. Hens cackled and scratched on the manure heaps and in the rickyard, cockerells crowed, and the ducks quacked. After milking, the cows gently meandered in an untidy procession to the meadow. Primrose, a roan cow, always took the lead. She was no bigger nor more aggressive than the others, nor did she appear to jockey for position, but she was always in the forefront.

We now had several calves. Beauty, who had been the first to calve, had presented us with twins, which was quite unusual. We took this to be a good augury for the future, but it was never repeated. Chloe, the sow, had farrowed well, and had reared eleven of her jolly little roly-poly piglets. These had already been marketed and we were hoping that her next effort would be equally successful.

Our hay crop had been a fair one, and now the corn was stooked in the field. I had helped with the stooking, but it was disappointing to find, after a windy night, that most of the stooks that I had handled, were laid flat. However, I found that there was really a knack in it. Once this was mastered, my stooks stood firm as any of the others. For three weeks the corn had to remain in the field—until the Church bells had rung for three Sundays—I was told.

Among the many hazards of our farming life was the weather. It had been unsettled for several weeks, and harvesting had been difficult. Now came torrential rain and everything became sodden. It rained almost without ceasing for several days. Then, one evening, we heard a sudden rushing sound. Looking from the kitchen door, we were horrified to see a swiftly flowing bubbling torrent of water sweeping across the yard, and racing along the side of the house. The river had overflowed, or burst its banks, and now seemed as if it might engulf us. We watched as the water spread as far as the door-step. The lawn at the front of the house became a lake, and the house was completely surrounded by water. Quickly we picked up rugs and pieces of light furniture and put them on the tables. Some we carried upstairs. We then made up a good fire and prepared to wait. Several times we looked out. The rush of water continued but still it had not risen above the door-steps.

When it was well past midnight, and the water by the house seemed to remain at the same level, John suggested that I should go to bed. He would remain up and would call me if necessary. I took a hot water bottle and went upstairs, but not to sleep. Still fully clothed, I lay under the eiderdown, listening with dismay to the rush and swirl of the water.

As soon as there was a glimmer of light, I looked out of the bath-room window. From here, I could see the meadow, deep in water. Along it ran a ridge of higher ground, and lined up along this I could see the shadowy shapes of the cows.

In the morning they splashed their way into their accustomed places in the cowshed. Milking was difficult, for the cows were nearly up to their udders in water. Fortunately the rain had stopped and almost imperceptibly the flood began to recede. We were most thankful that no water had entered the ground floor. The cellar was full, but that was of little consequence, as the only things stored there were a few spare jam jars and fruit bottles. These had been placed neatly on the thrall, but when the water had subsided, they lay, with some of them broken, in the smelly unpleasant residue left by the flood. Many buckets of water had to be pumped and much swilling and scrubbing done before the cellar was once more sweet and clean. I decided that for the future it should be left empty.

The water had reached above the top of the mens' wellingtons and John said he would have to supply them with thigh boots and other protective clothing if floods recurred. However, Loll said this was the worst he had ever known, and fortunately, we never again had one quite so severe.

My heart sank when I looked at the gardens. The kitchen garden was a sea of mud, and everything had been washed out of the herba-ceous border in the front. As the fowls had been already shut up in the roosts when the flood occurred, they did not suffer. They perched high and dry. With plenty of fresh strawy litter on the damp floor, they were quite comfortable. The ducks were jubilant. This new watery world was very much to their liking, and with their heads down and their tails aloft, they enjoyed to the full the succulent morsels they found in this new Paradise.

After the flood we had several days of close muggy weather. When the sheaves of corn should have been ready for carrying, they looked a sorry sight. The straw, which was golden when the corn was cut, had changed to a dreary grey. Because of the unfortunate weather, some of the corn in the ears had sprouted, and several of the sheaves carried a green topknot. The same amount of labour would be needed to harvest it, but the value of the crop was sadly diminished.

It was a long time before I could endure mishaps such as this, with equanimity. There was little purpose in fretting over something which could not be altered. But I often grieved when much time and hard labour was set at nought, by circumstances over which we had no control.

Soon after the flood, I had an attack of tonsilitis. My tempreature rose and I had to keep to my bed. Someone had to be found to do the household chores. In the nearby cottages was a girl who was under a cloud. She had committed what was considered by many to be an unforgivable offence. Rhoda had given birth to an illegitimate baby. Her home was really in the next village, but her highly respectable parents had been so horrified to learn that she was pregnant, that they had disowned her. The baby was born in the workhouse. After a very distressing time, Rhoda had found refuge with two middle aged spinsters in our village. More broad minded than most, they had offered her a home, and they doted on the baby, who was now six months old.

Rhoda earned what she could by doing domestic work daily, knowing that her baby was well looked after in her absence. We found, when she worked for us, that Rhoda was quietly efficient, and very reserved. We could not help wondering what had led to her fall from grace. In a roundabout way, we eventually learnt that it was the consequence of a party where the wine had flowed too freely. This was only hearsay and we never learnt any further details. Rhoda did not confide in us, nor I imagine in anyone, unless maybe to the Misses Elkins with whom she lived.

Rhoda came for part of each day, according to her other commitments, until I was well, when she then agreed to come for two mornings every week.

I was very glad of her help, for my odd jobs seemed to multiply. At busy times I helped with some of the farm work. Hay time I specially enjoyed. Whenever possible my lunch was packed with John's which I took to him when he was busy haymaking in the top fields. He had no time in the short respite at midday to come home for a meal.

As we ate, the men sat at a discreet distance from us, in the shade of the hedge, slicing great hunks of bread and cheese, with their clasp knives. It was as well not to think of the multifarious duties performed by these same knives, such as paunching rabbits and other unpleasant but necessary tasks. Liquid refreshment was usually cold tea, which the men brought in bottles.

How long the hay making took depended on the weather. Sometimes the turning and raking of the long swathes had to be repeated many times before the hay was dry. It was then carted and stored under the Dutch barn in the rick yard. If rain threatened, the hay was raked into cocks so that the inside, at least would be protected. This was one of the jobs in which I enjoyed helping.

# 21. *Winter pleasures*

I N THE WINTER the field work was not so exacting and we had time to visit our neighbours, and to entertain them in return. John was able to watch his favourite football team in Birmingham with his brother Stafford, and I could spend a pleasant Saturday afternoon with Cissie. It was on such an afternoon that a curious thing happened. Peggy was also visiting, and as we chatted, Cissie addressed me as Mrs John. Peggy suddenly said

"Why do you call her Mrs John, Cissie, why not Edith?"

"I don't think Edith suits her" said Cissie,

"Well, what name do you think would suit her," Peggy asked,

Without hesitation, Cissie said "Miriam."

Instantly, I was transported to Penny's cubicle at College, and the séance she held. Again I heard her say—

"You have a spirit guide named Miriam"

Why, out of the countless girls names that existed, should Cissie now choose this particular one? It was certainly strange and somewhat eerie.

Sometimes Ted and Cissie would invite us, together with several other friends for a musical evening. After a lavish meal, the singing began. I was generally the accompanist. Most of the songs were sentimental ballads such as 'Thora' and 'I hear you calling me.' From the men we had 'The Trumpeter' and similar old favourites. I soon knew the limited repertoires almost by heart. Each member contributed a solo, with great variety in the rendering of them. No discrimination was shown, all received the same applause. To my surprise, I found that John had quite a pleasant baritone voice. When pressed to sing, no excuses being allowed, he 'obliged' by singing some of my songs, which he knew well through frequent hearing.

Sometimes, after the music, the men would gather round the table for a gambling game of cards. They were all farmers considerably older than John. In the war years they had prospered, for prices of farm produce had risen steeply. Unfortunately, John had not shared this prosperity. On the other hand, all our equipment and stock had been bought at the inflated prices. As the stakes for which the men gambled were high, John and I usually left before the card playing began.

We did not yet possess a piano, so we could not invite friends for music, but we had some pleasant evenings playing Bridge. In the Autumn, John had a rabbiting party, which proved most popular, and became an annual event. The men, with their guns, gathered at the house in the morning, before setting off together. They took with them a large market basket in which I had packed their lunch of sandwiches, bread and cheese, small cakes and apples. There were also flasks of coffee and bottles of cider and beer.

Between other chores, I was busy most of the day preparing the evening meal for the men when they returned with their sharpened appetites. In the morning, I made some bread rolls, a fruit pie and a batch of jam tarts. A joint of beef had been cooked on the previous day, and a hen and other birds feathered and prepared. The hen was gently simmering on the hob. When cooked it was coated with white sauce and decorated. Then, into the oven, went the other birds to be roasted. John always tried to shoot a brace of pheasants for these occasions, but, if these were not forthcoming, we had ducks.

The men were fond of sherry trifle. When this was made, and the jacketed potatoes were slowly roasting in the bottom of the oven, the preparations were complete. Except for the potatoes the meal would be eaten cold.

In the afternoon Cissie came, and together we set the table, adding home-made pickles and chutney, beetroot and celery, cheese and biscuits to the well filled board.

It was dusk, before the men returned. Then there was much clatter and clanking of buckets, with great guffaws of laughter as they prepared themselves for the meal.

When their appetites were satisfied, they all relaxed, while Cissie and I cleared away. Then, out came the cards for the favourite games of 'Nap' and 'Farmers Glory.' The stakes were not high, and there was much merriment. A favourite expletive of one visitor was 'Dog bite me!' uttered whenever his luck was out. Often when an attempted score was not made, a derisory jingle would be sung to the loser. It was quite nonsensical, and was peculiar to the game, and possibly to this company, but it always produced laughter.

The party broke up as near as possible to midnight. That Sunday was the next day made no difference. Routine jobs such as feeding and milking had to be carried on whatever the day. Actually as the cowman had an occasional Sunday off, if often meant extra work for the 'boss.'

# 22. *Silly Geese?*

MUCH OF MY TIME was taken up by gardening, and in attending to the poultry. Among these I was most interested in the geese. In the November following the purchase of Jane and Susan, John bought a gander. As this happened on the 5th of the month, we named him Guy. It was often difficult to tell a gander from a goose, but there was no doubt about Guy. He was white, like the geese, but slightly bigger, with a lordly dignified air. When introduced to his two wives, his manner was somewhat condescending. Soon, I realized that he showed a preference for Susan. On the daily pere-grinations, Guy took the lead. Frequently Susan would walk by his side, but I never saw that privilege accorded to Jane.

Unfortunately, my admiration for the geese was not shared by John. I think he was beginning to regret having purchased them. He was most annoyed by the tiresome habit they had of pulling the ricks to pieces. As each straw was pulled from the rick, the grains of wheat fell from the ears, and were promptly picked up by the hens. The geese did not seeem to object to having their booty stolen. In fact their only delight seemed to be in pulling the straw. To prevent this, some stakes and wire were put to protect the ricks.

When Loll one day slipped from a rick, and injured himself quite badly on one of the stakes, I should not have been surprised if Susan, Jane and Guy had been summarily removed by John. However, although blamed for the accident, they still remained.

An old saying ran thus: "On Valentine's Day, every good duck and goose ought to lay." Susan and Jane were evidently good geese, for on this very day of the Spring following their purchase, Jane laid her first egg. Two days later Susan followed suit.

I had been advised not to try to hatch the first few that were laid, as they often proved infertile. From them, I made some mouth watering omelettes. The contents of one of the large eggs was enough to fill my omelette pan.

As they continued laying, I put four eggs under each broody hen that I managed to obtain, and put them securely in the small pens to be hatched. It would mean damping the nests frequently, but both eggs and hen would be safe from Chloe, or any other marauder.

Soon, I had several of the pens occupied. Each morning I let the hens off in turn. I was watching for the return of the last broody one morning when the geese crossed the yard. As usual Guy and Susan were in the forefront. Jane in the rear, passed close to the vacated pen. She saw the nest of goose eggs and stood for a moment as if transfixed; then she gave a loud Qu-a-a-rk! Guy and Susan halted. Jane again gave her loud cry and Guy came pattering back to her, followed by Susan. All three bent their long necks and looked at the eggs. They straightened up, and although I heard nothing, they appeared to be discussing the matter. Some conclusion was evidently reached, for Susan began to edge the eggs out of the nest with her beak. What would have happened I do not know for I could see the hen returning. I drove the geese away before they could alarm her, and then shut her safely on the nest.

The geese continued to lay, and as I had no more broodies, I decided to leave the goose eggs in the nest, hoping this might encourage the geese to sit, and hatch some goslings themselves. Jane and Susan had nests side by side in the roost. After laying an egg, each goose plucked from herself some fine down, with which to cover it. As the eggs increased, it was impossible to see them beneath their downy covering. Soon both geese showed a tendency to sit. Only eight more eggs had been laid and one goose could easily cover those. Then I had, what I thought was a capital idea. I would put the eight goose eggs in one nest, and put duck eggs in the other. A goose should be able to cover at least fifteen of these smaller eggs.

When Jane and Susan remained all day on their nests, I knew they were well broody, although they made no announcement of the fact, as the hens did, with their Cluck! Cluck! Cluck!

Taking advantage of their short absence from the roost, I carried out my plan one morning. The goose eggs were all put in one nest, the duck eggs in the other, all covered carefully with the down. I watched as Jane and Susan settled down again with apparent unconcern. Each morning Guy, the gander, accompanied them to the pond and back. He watched until they were safely settled on their nests again before leaving them to go on his solitary way.

During this time, Guy became very aggressive. He would approach one with loud hisses and outstretched neck, in a most menacing manner. Sometimes I heard the patter of his feet behind me, just in time to avoid an encounter. When I faced him, and spoke sharply, he retreated. I was happier when I had a stick to brandish, for he was always intimidated by this.

When the geese had been sitting for a fortnight, I examined the nests while they were absent. Jane's nest with the goose eggs was intact, but when I lifted the downy covering from the duck eggs I found it was sticky. To my surprise the duck eggs had dwindled to three. Here was a puzzle, no rat would dare brave the fury of a goose. Who, or what could be the thief. I determined to keep watch.

Several times, during the next few days, I peeped at intervals through the open roost door. The geese sat serene and comfortable. I knew that at the approach of a rat, or any other intruder, their voices would be raised in alarm.

At last, I found the culprit. One morning when I looked in, I was just in time to see Jane withdraw her head from beneath Susan. On her beak were the tell tale signs of the egg she had just eaten. Whether Susan had ever joined her in this nefarious feasting I never knew, but I thought not.

Next morning, I removed Susan's nest and only allowed Jane back into the roost, before shutting the door. I hoped that Susan would soon recover from her broodiness, and perhaps lay another clutch of eggs.

When the goose eggs under the hens were ready for the goslings to hatch, I found that, unlike chicks, they had great difficulty in emerging from the eggs. The shells were thick and the skin inside was tough. The effort of breaking through seemed to exhaust the baby goslings, and left to themselves, many would have died. First, I broke away a portion of the shell, and then gently tore back the tough skin, until the head was free. However carefully this was done bleeding occurred.

Having performed this office for the four eggs in one nest, I waited for the hen to return. The rather gory half hatched goslings were not a pretty sight. Unbelieving, the hen took one look. Then, with a great squawk of terror, she scuttled off, not to return. Surreptitiously the contents of the nest were placed under the other sitting hens This difficulty in hatching was no doubt bceause the eggs were too dry, although I had frequently damped the nests.

Jane hatched her brood with no trouble, but she had spent some time each morning on the pond and retained a lot of moisture in her feathers. Almost as soon as they were hatched, her greenish yellow, bright-eyed goslings, were led to the pond. Guy, proud father, walked in front, with Susan protecting the right-flank of the precious family, and Jane the left.

The goslings hatched by the hens were put in runs on the lawn, with the hens to mother them. Whenever the garden gate was left open, the geese would find their way in, and walk round the pens peering at the goslings as much as to say "They belong to us."

When the goslings were old enough to join the others, and became fully feathered, they were certainly a handsome sight and I shared Guy's pride as he strutted with dignity before his numerous progeny.

By Michaelmas the geese had grown big and fat, and some of them were sold. I was sad to see my flock depleted, but it was even worse when, just before Christmas, all, except the three stock birds, had to go. Before being marketed, they had to be rough plucked, which meant removing the big feathers, and most of the down. This was a time taking job with which our workmen's wives and some of their friends came to help.

The weather was cold, so on the first occasion, I let the women do this work in the kitchen. Soon the small particles of down were dancing in the air like snowflakes. In spite of the closed doors they seemed to float into almost every corner of the house.

Each of the women had a sack bag on her lap. On this the goose was placed, with its neck over her left arm. One had just been arranged in this fashion, when, from the goose came a loud Qu-a-ark! The woman jumped to her feet with a cry of alarm. Feathers and down flew in all directions. When everyone had been convinced that the bird was really dead, and that the noise must have been the result of an air lock in its gullet, there was a lot of laughter, and after some of the innumerable 'cuppas' the work was at last resumed.

Besides the cash, my geese provided us with some superbly soft down cushions. and eventually with a luxurious down bed.

Susan, Jane and Guy had been with us for several years, when one Spring morning I noticed Susan standing alone and immobile in the yard. This was unusual, and as I watched she suddenly keeled over, and was unable to regain her feet. As she lay and fluttered helplessly, I wondered what to do. The men were all at work in the top fields, but I decided to go for help. Scurrying along the lane as fast as I could, I at last saw John and beckoned to him. He came saying "Whatever is the matter?"

"It's the goose, John" I said, "It's Susan. She's ill."

"Good gracious, is that all" said John "I thought the house must be on fire."

He came back with me to the farm, but when we got there, Susan was dead. John thought she must have been egg bound, as she had shown no sign of illness. He carried her and laid her for the time being in a corner of the stable.

That night when Jane had gone to roost, Guy stood at the roost door and called plaintively for Susan. He gave a continual hoarse cry, unlike any I had heard from him before. It sounded like Gah-aa! Dah-aa! He called until it became dark, and the roost door was shut, repeating his melancholy lament on several successive nights.

We replaced Susan with another goose, which we named Alice, but Guy treated her with apparent indifference, content to let her walk behind him with Jane.

How the expression "Silly goose" arose I cannot imagine, for my geese seemed to me to possess considerable intelligence.

# 23. *Maternity*

During our third Spring at the farm I found to my delight that I was pregnant. We had now been married nearly five years, and I had begun to despair of ever having the family, which I so ardently desired. When I told John the good news, he did not receive it with the enthusiasm that I had anticipated. I was most disappointed, and longed for him to share my glad excitement. He was as delighted, I knew, as I was myself, but it was not John's way to give vent to his feelings. How I wished that for once, he would enthuse with me. Why, I wondered, had he become so apathetic? What had changed the merry, carefree youth I had known, into this grave and unemotional husband of mine? Did the things he had endured and the sights he had seen during the war, still occupy his mind, or was it the persistent headaches which had since afflicted him that were responsible for his lack of enthusiasm.

Although his placid acceptance of circumstances lacked zest, I wondered if John's frame of mind might not have certain advantages. If he never rose to peaks of jubilant anticipation, he was no doubt spared much disappointment and disillusion. So often my mercurial mind had raised me to dizzy heights of expectation, from whence I had descended with a bump, into the dull valley of reality.

Now, my precious secret, like a singing bird, was ever present, as I went about my daily chores. Only with intimate friends would it be shared. To Dash and Winifred the glad news was sent, but I had barely received their letters of congratulation and delight, when I had certain ominous symptoms, which showed that all was not well.

When the doctor was called, he looked very grave, and said I should have to exercise great care, or there would be a recurrence of my former mishap. After an enforced rest in bed, there must be no heavy work.

This posed a problem. Who, I wondered, would carry out my multifarious duties? Rhoda had no more time to spare, but she found a little maid for me, Florrie, who had just left school. She would live in, for a wage of six shillings a week. Rhoda instructed her in those routine household chores which she was able to do, and my outside jobs were relegated to the men.

When I was once more able to help with the lighter work, time hung less heavily. The knitting and sewing of the layette proved a pleasurable way of relieving the tedium, but it was irksome to see my once neat garden in the front of the house becoming neglected. Much that should have been consigned to the compost heap, or bonfire, still languished there unbeautifully. John disliked gardening, and the men had no time to spend on flower borders.

Inevitably the months passed. A few days before the baby was due, Mrs Parsons arrived. She was the monthly nurse who always attended John's family, and their relatives, when her services were required. Mrs Parsons was a widow. Her age appeared to be in the late forties. She was trim and well corseted, with quick glancing eyes, dark hair, and a thin lipped mouth. Soon she had Florrie running hither and thither, fetching and carrying for her, and I realized that her capability as a midwife, did not extend to the field of domestic chores.

When Mrs Parsons had been with us for two days, she roused John early one morning, and asked him to fetch the doctor, who lived three miles away. There was no telephone in our part of the village, John's quickest means of transport was by bicycle. To me, it seemed hours before the doctor arrived; each moment was a horror of pain, with nothing to alleviate it. How could a beneficient God permit such agony in the performance of a natural function, I wondered.

When, at last, the baby was born, and they told me it was a girl, my first thought was 'Poor lamb, one day she too may have to go through this hell.'

Mrs Parsons had little sympathy. She firmly believed that children were conceived in sin, and that the suffering of childbirth was the penalty one must pay.

Although feeling somewhat diffident about coping with the baby alone, I was not sorry to see Mrs Parsons depart, nor, I am sure, was Florrie.

After much indecision, John and I had decided that the baby's name should be Joy. Many lovely names we had discarded, because they were often subjected to an unlovely abbreviation. In fulfilment of a promise made many years before, she would also bear the name of Winifred.

I could scarcely believe that my long standing dream had at last materialised. This adorable scrap of humanity was really my own. As I cuddled her in my arms, all pain, discomfort and frustration, were forgotten, in wonder at the miracle.

Joy was a good baby and this was fortunate. Time was not elastic, and before her advent, the days seemed fully occupied. Now, the work had not diminished. My outside duties were resumed, but the happiest part of the day was, for me, the time spent on satisfying the needs of the baby.

Florrie was proving quite a capable maid, willing and anxious to learn. She was particularly interested in cooking, and eager to become proficient. My willingness to teach her, proved my undoing, for it was not long before Florrie found herself a situation in Birmingham as a cook. She not only earned more money but was able to find more entertainment and companionship in town, than was possible in our somewhat isolated farmhouse.

Florrie came occasionally to visit Joy, of whom she had become quite fond, and on one occasion brought her a large talking doll, a sign of her new affluence.

When Joy was two years old, I again became pregnant and was delighted at the thought of a companion for her. Fervently I hoped that we might have a son. Most men, I knew, were proud to have a son to carry on the family name and to follow their own occupation, but the choice was beyond our control.

Once again I nearly ran into disaster. One day Stafford John's brother, told us that he wanted to buy some more cattle. His Father had been in poor health for some time and Stafford now managed the Dunton farm. There was to be a sale of Irish cattle at Bridgnorth, which he wished to attend. This would entail quite a long journey, John agreed to go with Stafford and he suggested that I should also go with them. I welcomed the idea. Outings were few and far between. A long ride through a new country side would be a pleasure indeed, especially as the trees were already tinged by Autumn.

All went well till we reached the town, which none of us had visited before. Ted, our neighbour had come with us but the district was also new to him.

To find the cattle market, the men thought it would be a good idea to follow some driven cattle. Unfortunately, the drovers took a short cut which led up a very steep hill, at the bottom of which was a river. Many cars were poor climbers, and ours was no exception. As we neared the top of the hill, the car began to run backwards. This behaviour always alarmed me, but when I thought of the river at the foot of the hill, I was terrified. When the brakes eventually held, I was out of the car almost before it stopped. By the time it was re-started, I had reached the top of the hill.

My day passed pleasantly. It was a new experience to have so much leisure, in which to window shop and wander around, for I did not meet the men until it was time to return. They, too, had enjoyed the day, and Stafford had bought the cattle he wanted, so we all started the long journey home in a very happy mood.

When we had been travelling for some time, I needed to 'spend a penny.' Such things were never mentioned, the idea of asking John to stop the car for such a purpose with other men present, was un-thinkable. The idea shocked my modesty, so with discomfort, I contained myself.

Whether it was this, or the fright on the hill, or perhaps the motion of the car, I do not know, but when we reached home, I was quite unwell. The doctor prescribed the same old routine of rest and care if I was to save the baby.

We decided that Florrie must be replaced by another school leaver, and Ada came. She was clumsy and awkward. Noise followed in her wake, doors banged, china crashed, and she always seemed the centre of commotion. Thankfully, I said 'Goodbye' to Ada, and Minnie was engaged. She was certainly quieter and more helpful than Ada, but a poor substitute for Florrie.

In due course Mrs Parsons arrived again. Things were no easier than before, but fate was kind, and we had a son, a bonny healthy boy weighing nearly ten pounds. He was named William after his grandfather. As soon as Mrs Parsons arrived, Joy had been despatched to Dunton to stay. Here we thought she would be quite happy with her grandparents, her uncles and aunties. Such, however, was not the case, for when Joy had been there for barely a week, she was brought home. Apparently she had worried them each day to be taken back to Mummy. Finally, Joy had stuffed her nightie into her small suit-case, and Grandma found her trying to drag it downstairs.She was going home, Joy said, with Uncle Bob, as she affectionately called the milkman, who collected our milk, as well as that from Dunton.

Such determination gained her point and she came home, only to find that an interloper had taken her place. We had tried in every possible way to prepare her for the coming of the baby, but it was quite evident that Joy was jealous and resented his presence.

When Mrs Parsons had gone, I let Joy help me when the baby was bathed, allowed her to fetch and carry various things for his toilet, until the jealousy and resentment vanished. Then to everyone who came, she proudly announced the fact that she had a baby brother.

## 24. *Foot and Mouth*

THINGS HAD JUST about reverted to normal after the birth of William, when we received an unexpected devastating blow. There was an outbreak of foot and mouth disease in the country, but there was no case anywhere near us. However, as a precaution, John took out an insurance policy. One morning he came in from the milking looking so dejected that I exclaimed "Whatever is the matter John" "I believe," said he "That we have a case of 'Foot and Mouth': One of the calves is slobbering: I don't like the look of it at all. As soon as I have had my breakfast, I will fetch the vet." The vet came, and confirmed John's surmise. We were horrified, and most distressed. To lose our herd, which John had carefully built up over the years would be a tragedy, and we knew that all would now have to perish. It had taken time, discrimination, and much culling and replacing to get together the cows which now filled the sheds. All this effort was to vanish in smoke—literally in smoke, for all would have to be burnt. The pigs, too, would share the same fate, for anything with a cloven hoof was likely to incur the fell disease.

The following weeks were full of horror. Men came, and dug a great ditch in the meadow at the back of the house. To the brink of this, the cows were led, and despatched quickly with a humane killer. I refused to witness any of the preparations, and when the carcases were burnt, the mere thought of the holocaust gave me nightmares. Pungent, acrid smoke filled the atmosphere and a stupid little jingle of childhood's days kept coming into my mind. It ran—

> 'The gentle cow all red, and white,
> I love with all my heart.
> She gives me cream, with all her might,
> To eat with apple tart.'

No more cream should we have from our gentle cows, many of whom we knew by name. Topsy, Myrtle, Nan, and Sue had gone with the others, to their untimely grave.

A policeman was stationed outside the farm and all unauthorized entrance forbidden. When I took the children out in the pram, my feet and the pram wheels had to be thoroughly disinfected. With no visitors allowed, we felt very isolated, and, to me, the empty cow-sheds and pigsties seemed haunted. Often in the early morning I heard in imagination, the clank of the buckets, and the rattle of chains, but the meticulous cleaning and disinfecting which ensued deterred any bovine ghost from returning.

To add to our misfortune, the insurance company that John had chosen, went bankrupt on the receipt of our claim, so instead of recompense, we lost our premiums, as well as the solicitor's fees.

From the government, we received some compensation, but only carcase value. Of course our income from the milk had ceased. We were not allowed to re-stock for some time, and for that period, the sight of the empty sheds caused our spirits to sink to a very low level, which the somewhat melancholy situation of the "Hollies" did nothing to alleviate.

By ones and twos, the cows were eventually replaced. To me, they remained merely replacements. They had not the individuality of those we had lost, some of which had been reared from birth. Occasionally I had milked an odd cow, just to keep my hand in, but this no longer had any appeal.

Fortunately, as time passed, we were spared any further dramas of flood or pestilence. Each year the river rose and flooded the meadows, and sometimes the cowsheds, but never again to the same extent as on the first occasion. Often, however, it was necessary for the men to wear the waterproof thigh boots with which John had provided them.

Footwear for the children proved a problem. Nothing that was obtainable was really serviceable for conditions such as ours. The ubiquitous wellingtons were not yet made for tiny feet. When William was able to toddle around the yard on his own, like most children, he loved to play with water. If there was a puddle, he

found it, and there was usually one somewhere. When he was retrieved, shoes and socks were often sodden, and needed constant
replacement.

When Annie, my sister, paid us one of her infrequent visits, I
asked her how she coped with this difficulty. She was now the mother
of two sturdy boys and the farm where they lived was usually very
muddy in the winter. Practical Annie had found a solution and her
boys wore clogs, which kept their feet warm and dry. I thought
this a sensible idea, but I did not adopt it. It was hard to imagine the
tiny feet of dainty little Joy encased in such unyielding clumsy footwear, even though she often joined William in his watery escapades.

# 25. *The Decision*

Vᴵsɪᴛs ᴛᴏ ᴍʏ home in Lewes had of necessity been few, but each of the babies had been taken in turn to be introduced to their grandparents. Frequent letters kept me in touch with all the family news. Each Saturday morning I posted my weekly budget so that it would be delivered on Sunday morning. This sometimes presented difficulties, but I knew that there would be concern and disappointment if the letter should not arrive home at the usual time.

Mother's heart condition had not improved, and most of her time was spent in bed. She was often in great pain, so after a particularly disturbing letter from Father, I paid a fleeting visit home. With her indomitable spirit, Mother spoke of her future plans. The very effort of speaking taxed her to the utmost. It was with a sinking heart that I realized her frailty.

Although I knew it could not long be delayed, the news of Mother's death when it came, was still a shock. I felt denuded, and as if my own hold on life had become more tenuous. The solid and dependable buttress of my childhood had crumbled.

After Mother's death, Father paid frequent visits to each one of the family. On one of these occasions when he was about to visit the "Hollies", Stanley's wife Margaret wrote to ask if Peggy her small daughter could also come. Peggy was on holiday because her school had been closed for an epidemic. She was missing her play mates and had not been very well. Peggy was an attractive child with tight blonde curls and very blue eyes. She was a year older than Joy, who was wildly excited at the thought of her coming. Father broke his journey in London, where he collected Peggy, and they duly arrived. The children had a wonderful time with Grandpa, who enjoyed their company, and was ever ready to entertain them, when their own resources failed.

The visit was almost at an end, when I woke one morning with a very sore throat. Thinking it was the onset of one of my usual attacks of tonsilitis, I determined to say nothing, if possible, till Peggy and Grandpa had gone. Feeling far from well, it was with relief that I saw them depart.

Next day, when I sought the cause of an itching, which had suddenly become unbearble, I found a spate of small spots. Could it be Scarlet Fever? When I looked at my tongue I was almost sure. The doctor confirmed it, and made arrangements for me to be taken to the fever hospital some fifteen miles away. I could not be nursed at home or the sale of milk would have to stop. We soon discovered that Scarlet Fever was the epidemic which had closed Peggy's school, and which she had unwittingly conveyed to me.

The small hospital to which I was taken had a rural situation, and was surrounded by extensive grounds, but it was not until the fever had left me, that I realized how pleasant was the environment, in which I was to spend six whole weeks. It was not long before I was wishing with all my heart that I could be outside in this heavenly month of May. Each day the sun shone, the birds twittered and sang, and the repetitive cuckoo called without ceasing. As dusk fell, a nightingale poured out his enchanting liquid notes; now and again an owl hooted.

Soon my wish was granted and each day my bed was wheeled on to the terrace. This was bliss indeed, and I should have been completely content, if I had not been disturbed by a niggly feeling of guilt. Was I an unnatural wife and mother to feel so serene, when separated from my home and family. For consolation, I comforted myself with the thought that no amount of fretting, or chafing, would aid my recovery, or hasten my return.

Though I had been assured as to their well being, I had a sudden urgent desire to see the children. Visits from them were prohibited; even when John came, we only saw each other through a window. Near the opposite window, in the side wall against which my bed was placed, ran the boundary fence of the hospital. This was about six feet high. One day I suggested to John that he might bring the children here and hoist them up, so that I might at least see their faces.

This he did, but it proved disastrous to my peace of mind. I was over-whelmed by home sickness, and it was several days before I recovered from depression and loss of appetite.

As I became more mobile, I wondered how to occupy myself. Matron had told me how the weedy garden troubled her. The elderly gardener was unable to cope adequately with the extensive grounds, and she had tried in vain to get the nurses interested. Soon, with the gardener's permission, I spent a part of each day slowly but happily plying hoe and rake, viewing with satisfaction the weed free surfaces.

On rainy days, of which fortunately there were few, I found various little ways in which I could help the nurses, although they were not overworked, and often had time for a chat.

Between the wards was a small kitchen, which had a cooking range, in which a bright fire was kept burning. Here, with eggs provided by John, the other ingredients supplied by the nurses, I made them an occasional sponge cake. The time was chosen care-fully, the whole operation surrounded by secrecy. No sooner was the cake made than it was consumed with glee, and the utensils removed from sight. The air of conspiracy added flavour to the proceedings. Would Matron have frowned? I never knew, for the secret was well kept.

There were no other adult patients in the hospital. Much of my time was spent alone, with leisure to think about many things. I mused upon the ten years which had elapsed since we had entered the "Hollies" with such high hopes. How many of those hopes had come to fruition? What was the sum total of achievement? Two healthy endearing children were a visible asset, but it seemed that the scales hung low on the debit side.

Our financial situation was still precarious. Foot and Mouth had been a severe setback. Since the outbreak there had been an ominous fall in prices. The depression which was soon to overtake the whole country, was already spreading its insidious tentacles. Our years of unremitting toil had gathered no harvest, but we were luckier than some. Several of John's farming friends who, like us, had started on their own after the war had been reduced to bankruptcy.

On the physical side, neither John nor I were as fit as we had been. Worry and responsibility had done nothing to mitigate John's headaches, and his arm, which had been injured by shrapnel during the war, often gave trouble. He was no longer the happy carefree

John of old, but seemed to have lost the faculty for enjoyment, and had become serious and often moody.

Our mental processes I felt had become almost moribund. There was little beyond 'the common round, the trivial task' to offer any stimulus. After long days spent in the strenuous physical work of the farm, one became comatose, even prolonged conversation was an effort.

Day followed day with its inevitable routine. Sunday, far from being a day of rest, was usually one of extra exertion, for my little maid, and each of the men in turn, had Sunday off.

We had few visitors, but Ted and Cissie often came. Of late, I had noticed that when they were with us, there was a curious tension in their attitude to one another, and Cissie was strangely quiet and unlike her usual self. When Cissie came alone for a cup of tea, she was most garrulous, and entertained me with intimate details about her friends and their domestic affairs, but she never mentioned her own. I often wondered, if the relationship between Cissie and her husband was a happy one, but as to this she gave me no clue.

As I pondered over the lines into which our lives had fallen, I felt that we were in a rut. Was this to be the ultimate pattern of our lives? Were we always to be so encumbered by the irksome, mundane duties, that our vision would be clouded, the pleasure and satisfaction of our farming life lost. Even living, as it were, among the grass roots, surely it was not necessary to become a cabbage.

My thoughts ran in circles, as I wondered what could be done to effect a change. I eventually came to the conclusion that the one thing that might be changed was our environment. A more salubrious situation might prove beneficial in more ways than one. The very idea of such a move filled me with excitement, but the difficulty would be in getting John to agree. He disliked change. Even the re-arrangement of our furniture annoyed him, so I guessed that it would be a major problem to get him to consent to such an upheaval, even supposing a suitable farm could be found.

I thought of various ways in which I could put the suggestion to John, so that it would really make an impact, and he would not dismiss it, as merely an unsettled feeling on my part, due to the fever.

Eventually I wrote a letter which was quite out of character. It was one long complaint about conditions at the farm. I was not given to complaining. On the principle that "What can't be cured must be endured"; the many difficulties had either been overcome or accepted.

Now, I managed to find a formidable list of disadvantages, the floods, the lack of electricity or gas, the interminable task of pumping and carrying the endless buckets of water, I listed all these as well as the other amenities that were missing. Finally, I mentioned my recurring attacks of tonsilitis, which were undoubtedly due to the low, damp situation, which I was sure would eventually undermine the health of us all. The "Hollies" could not possibly be a good place in which to bring up the children, so would John please try to find a farm with, at least, a more salubrious situation.

I waited anxiously for John's reply. The tone of my letter must have surprised him. I knew only too well that John was very hard to persuade against his own wishes. If he once vetoed the suggestion, the project would remain a forlorn hope. Perhaps he would casually dismiss the whole idea. Then, when it had lain dormant for a while, it might be brought to life as a new idea of his own.

I was used to this habit of John's. I had learnt to be patient, knowing that, given time, most of my suggestions would eventually be carried out. But I was not willing for the idea of a move to be buried, and exhumed at a later date. Suddenly I was all impatience for something to be done speedily. Supposing John was unwilling, then I must find another solution. However knotty the problem, I was determined to find an answer. In imagination I had already turned the last page on the chapter of our life at the "Hollies."

At last John's reply came. Nurse brought the letter to me while I was still in bed. Eagerly anticipated it had been, but now, as I held it in my hand, I had a strange disinclination to open it. Would the answer be "Yea" or "Nay?" I knew the dilemma in which I should be placed, if it proved to be negative. So much of our life at the "Hollies" had appeared in review to be negative, that this might finally tip the scale, and our marriage itself be in jeopardy.

With hesitant fingers, I split open the envelope and removed the letter, which was a long one. The contents surprised and relieved me. Without prevarication, John agreed with all my findings, and was willing to move. In fact, on receipt of my letter he had at once started enquiries. By sheer good luck, he had heard of a farm that would soon be available. It was about five miles from the "Hollies." John had already contacted the owner, an elderly farmer who was about to retire. He knew John, and was willing to consider him as a tenant. The Church and the village shop were not far from the house, which stood on a small hill. John hoped I should like the house and situation as much as he liked the look of the land.

By the time I had finished reading the letter, my spirits had soared. I was already painting the future with roseate hues. Now I could hardly wait for my release from hospital. The short time that still remained seemed never ending, but at last the day of departure arrived. When Matron and the nurses had been thanked for their kindness and consideration, I was soon on my way home. The children received me with hugs and kisses: in no time at all it seemed as if I had never been away!

Next morning, as soon as breakfast was over, John and I set out together to view the promised land. The sun shone. The sky was blue. Wild roses and honeysuckle twined in the hedges. Here and there some stately foxgloves reared their purple heads. My heart felt as light as the birds which twittered and carolled around us.

Soon the long low farmhouse came into view bathed in sunshine. As we drove into the yard a shaggy dog came towards us barking furiously. Sensing that we were not marauders he accompanied us to the door, with a gently wagging tail. We were received by Mr Lucas, a short stout man with bushy eyebrows and a full beard. With his left hand he continually brushed the lapels of his coat in a vain endeavour to remove the snuff with which it was impregnated. We were shown over the house. Then, as John and Mr Lucas discussed farm matters, my mind was busy with the thought of the improvements we would endeavour to make when this became our home. Many months would have to elapse before this became possible, but there would be much to occupy us in the meantime. I was delighted with what I had already seen of the house and farm. It was good to think that here no polluted river would rush relentlessly through cowsheds and barn. No misty miasma would veil these meadows which now lay bathed in sunshine. I had to remind myself that all was now looking its best on this radiant June day. Life would never be a continual summer but as we started on our homeward way I viewed the future with hope. Here in these 'fresh fields and pastures new' we should be able to begin a brighter and possibly a more auspicious chapter of our lives.